KALIGHAT

The most famous Śākta Temple in India

THE ŚĀKTAS

An Introductory and Comparative Study

ERNEST A. PAYNE
B.A., B.D. (London), B.Litt. (Oxford)

DOVER PUBLICATIONS, INC.
Mineola, New York

Published in Canada by General Publishing Company, Ltd., 30 Lesmill Road, Don Mills, Toronto, Ontario.

Published in the United Kingdom by Constable and Company, Ltd., 3 The Lanchesters, 162–164 Fulham Palace Road, London W6 9ER.

Bibliographical Note

This Dover edition, first published in 1997, is an unabridged republication of the work first published by Oxford University Press in 1933.

Library of Congress Cataloging-in-Publication Data

Payne, Ernest A. (Ernest Alexander), 1902–1980.
The Saktas : an introductory and comparative study / Ernest A. Payne.
p. cm.
Reprint. Originally published: London : Oxford University Press, 1933.
Includes bibliographical references and index.
ISBN 0-486-29866-3 (pbk.)
I. Title.
BL1282.24.P39 1997
294.5'514—dc21 97-24965
CIP

Manufactured in the United States of America
Dover Publications, Inc., 31 East 2nd Street, Mineola, N.Y. 11501

PREFACE

THIS study was embarked upon at the suggestion of the late Dr. J. N. Farquhar, to whom all those interested in Indian religion owe so much. But for his generous help and encouragement it would never have reached its present form. It is intended merely as an introduction to the subject, based upon the literature already available in Europe.

It is difficult to be consistent in the transliteration of Indian words, particularly when authors are quoted who vary greatly in the systems they adopt. In general an effort has been made to follow the scheme used by Dr. Farquhar in his *Outline of the Religious Literature of India.*

I am indebted to many friends who have drawn my attention to books, read the MS., and helped in other ways. Special thanks are due to Dr. Edward Thompson, of Oxford; the Rev. W. Sutton Page, of the London School of Oriental Studies; and the Rev. E. C. Dewick, of Calcutta. Marburg is making a name for itself among German universities for its interest in Comparative Religion. Much of the work for this book was done there.

In dealing with this subject I have endeavoured to keep in mind the words of the Apostle Paul, which form the motto of Regent's Park College, where I received a part of my training: 'Prove all things; hold fast that which is good.'

E.A.P.

TABLE OF CONTENTS

LIST OF ILLUSTRATIONS

ABBREVIATIONS

AJT	*American Journal of Theology.*
BRLS	Thompson and Spencer: *Bengali Religious Lyrics, Śākta.*
EHI	V. A. Smith: *Early History of India.*
Ency. Brit	*Encyclopædia Britannica.*
ERE	*Encyclopædia of Religion and Ethics.*
HBLL	D. C. Sen: *History of Bengali Language and Literature.*
HDB	Hastings: *Dictionary of the Bible.*
HSI	Glasenapp: *Heilige Stätten Indiens.*
JAOS	*Journal of the American Oriental Society.*
JASB	*Journal of the Asiatic Society of Bengal.*
JRAS	*Journal of the Royal Asiatic Society.*
OHI	V. A. Smith: *Oxford History of India.*
ORLI	Farquhar: *Outline of the Religious Literature of India.*
SBE	*Sacred Books of the East*
SS	Woodroffe: *Shakti and Shākta.*
TT	Avalon: *Tantrik Texts.*
ZTK	*Zeitschrift fūr Theologie and Kircke.*

CHAPTER I

INTRODUCTION

MANY elements in Indian religion have been neglected, or adversely criticised, simply because they have been distasteful to Western students, and although no real effort has been made to understand them. Rabindranath Tagore, in one of his latest and wisest books, *Creative Unity*, reminds us that 'when a stranger from the West travels in the Eastern world he takes the facts that displease him and readily makes use of them for his rigid conclusions, fixed upon the unchallengeable authority of his personal experience. It is like a man who has his own boat for crossing his village stream, but, on being compelled to wade across some strange watercourse, draws angry comparisons, as he goes, from every patch of mud and every pebble which his feet encounter.' Such an attitude can be charged with all too much truth against many of those who have written of Hinduism.

Śāktism is one of the phases of Indian religion which has received much condemnation and abuse; it is also one of the phases which has been little studied. Writers have been content to follow one another in expressions of disgust, rather than embark on the difficult task of examining it. In the account of the Śāktas given by Hopkins, for example, words like 'obscenity', 'bestiality', 'pious profligacy' frequently occur, and he tells us that 'a description of the different rites would be to reduplicate an account of indecencies of which the least vile is too esoteric to sketch faithfully.' Language almost equally violent is to be found in the pages of William Ward, the Abbé Dubois, H. H. Wilson, Monier Williams, Barth, William Crooke and many lesser known writers. Yet throughout India, and particularly in Bengal, there are hundreds of thousands of Śāktas, and they are the product of one of the most important and widespread movements within Hinduism, a movement which, however dark some of its expressions may be, has produced some remarkable types of genuine piety, and a considerable literature, and which has in recent times had able apologists.

We are coming increasingly to realise that 'no error has ever spread widely that was not the exaggeration or perversion of a truth.' If we would convince men of the inadequacy of their religious conceptions, and the harmful results of their religious practices, we must first seek to understand and appreciate the ways in which they have expressed their experiences, and without hesitating to condemn, where we feel that to be necessary, we must use what truth may be there as a stepping-stone to something higher. However crude, superstitious and repellent Śāktism may be on certain of its sides, it must be studied if it is to be combated effectually.

The numerous *Tantras* form the chief literature of the sect. Until 1913 none of these had appeared in translation in the West, and even in India it was not till about 1900 that the first English version of a *Tantra* was published. Of late years, however, a Western apologist for Śāktism has issued a series of works which have prepared the way for a more scientific study of the movement. Translations of *Tantras*, works on Śākta *yoga*, and general introductions to different phases of the subject have since 1913 come fast from the pen of a certain Arthur Avalon. Sir John Woodroffe has now acknowledged himself as chiefly responsible for these books, but as he was assisted by another writer, who prefers to remain anonymous, it seems better to quote sometimes Avalon and sometimes Woodroffe, according to the name on the title-page of the work in question, rather than to ascribe everything to the latter. Unfortunately, these books are far from easy to read; they are badly written, and are largely uncritical in method. The zeal of a convert often runs away with his judgment. Woodroffe refers in one of his works to his 'strong bent towards the clear and accurate statement of facts,'[1] but he is obviously interested far less in the history

[1] *SS*, p. 39.

and development of ideas, far less in their truth, than in the meaning attached to them today by the average sincere and intelligent worshipper. Students of Indian religion, however, owe him a great debt for having opened up this important and difficult field. What he has already accomplished may be seen by comparing the older accounts of the Śāktas with those of Helmuth von Glasenapp in his various books on Hinduism, or with that from the pen of Sten Konow in the new edition of Chantepie de la Saussaye's *Lehrbuch der Religionsgeschichte*. Both Glasenapp and Konow make frequent use of Avalon's *Tantrik Texts*. Another German scholar, Heinrich Zimmer, has attempted to explain Indian ritual art in general by means of the principles laid down in these *Tantras*.

This changed attitude is due almost entirely to the publications of Arthur Avalon. A beginning has also been made, however, with the translation of Śākta poetry, and new and rich material is placed at the disposal of the Western student.

The three chief characteristics of Śāktism are its idea of the Deity as Destroyer, its conception of God as Mother, and its attention to ceremonial. Each of these features can be paralleled in other forms of Hinduism, but nowhere are they so combined and emphasised as in this sect.

The word *Śakti* means 'energy.' Power or Force is conceived as the active principle in the universe, and is personified as a goddess. From the primordial *Śakti* every other form of activity proceeds. Under many different names it is worshipped as *Devī* or the Mother. In its cult, it must be confessed at once, it has been connected with what has been generally and, in the main, rightly regarded as the most debased side of Hinduism. The worshipper seeks to obtain 'power' by the most varied means. It has been, in many places, a religion of blind terror, of uncomprehended forces, of the terrible mystery of life and death. Awe, dread, propitiation have been its characteristic notes. Yet tenderness and love have also been present, and only these words can be used to express the attitude of many Śāktas to their goddess. Side by side with the abominations of Śāktism we have to set the poems of the great eighteenth century poet Rām Prasād. The first stage in the conversion of Rāmakṛishṇa (1833-86), the famous Bengali saint and mystic, came when he began to frequent the temple of Kālī (one of the best known of the more terrible forms of the goddess) at Dakshinesvara, and although he passed through various phases, in which Vaishṇavas, Muhammadans and Christians influenced him, yet he always regarded Kālī as the chief manifestation of God, and as the Divine Mother of the Universe, and before her idols he worshipped. The influence of Śākta ideas, mediated probably by Rāmakṛishṇa, can also be traced in the references to God as Mother to be found in the writings and addresses of Keshub Chunder Sen (1838–84), and the Swami Vivekānanda (1862–1902). The same line of thought continues in the writings of Sister Nivedita, the enthusiastic disciple of Vivekānanda, and in a different direction, though quite distinctly, in that curious one-time Roman Catholic, Brahmabandhav Upadhyaya (1861–1907).[1]

The appeal which Śākta ideas have made to men and women like these has been insufficiently recognised. Nor has the more philosophical side of the sect received due attention. 'God is worshipped as the Great Mother,' says Woodroffe, 'because in this aspect God is active, and produces, nourishes and maintains all. But this is for worship. God is no more female than male or neuter. God is beyond sex . . . the Power or active aspect of God the immanent is called Śakti. In her static transcendent aspect the Mother, or Śakti, is Śiva or the Good. That is, philosophically speaking, Śiva is the unchanging Consciousness and Śakti is its changing Power appearing as mind and matter.'[2] Such philosophical justification for certain Śākta beliefs can be found in the *Tantras*, as well as in more modern works like the *Principles of Tantra*, which Avalon has translated and edited. In Śāktism, indeed, as elsewhere in Hinduism, we have two orders of religion living side by side. They are mutually tolerant, indeed each assumes the other to be a phase of itself; one is philosophic, the other popular; one universalistic, the other local; one spiritual, the other magical.

[1] For a useful and attractive account of Brahmabandhav see Friedrich Heiler, *Christlicher Glaube und indisches Geistesleben*, pp. 51–79.

[2] *SS*, p. 8 f. Cp. Glasenapp, *Brahma und Buddha*, p. 155.

Too often Western writers have concentrated their attention on the second. Yet it is equally unsatisfactory to look only at the higher side. The sect has had most of its adherents among the more primitive peoples of India. Nowhere have the sexual emotions been more deliberately exploited in the name of religion, nowhere have the animal instincts and dark imaginings of early man been given greater scope. Śāktism is a movement as complex as any within Hinduism. We propose first of all to describe the sect, and to outline its practices; then to consider the rise of Śākta ideas in the religious literature of Hinduism. An attempt will be made to indicate some of the possible causes of its popularity, and the origin of some of its beliefs. The background in Bengal and Assam will then be filled in in greater detail, for only with that background in mind are we in a position to understand the fine examples of intense devotion and touching faith to be found among the Śāktas. Moreover, it is this background which helps to explain the close connection in certain places between Śāktism and some of the extremer phases of the modern Nationalist movement. Finally, with the object of the better understanding of the sect, some comparisons with other systems of belief and practice will be made.

CHAPTER II

THE CULT OF THE GODDESS

THE boundaries and extent of the sect are difficult to determine. The female energy of any deity in the Hindu pantheon may be worshipped, and one can trace Śākta ideas not only in Hinduism but also in Jainism and Buddhism. As an organised sect, however, Śāktism is linked closely with Śaivism, and the goddess is regarded as one of the many forms of the consort of Śiva. The abundance of names and epithets is, at first, somewhat confusing, but they enshrine within them much of the history of the movement. 'Just as Śiva has 1,008 names or epithets,' says Monier Williams, 'so his wife possesses a feminine duplicate of nearly every one of his designations. At least one thousand distinct appellations are assigned to her, some expressive of her benignant, some of her ferocious character.'[1] Among those that most frequently occur are Kālī, the dark goddess, whose name came to be connected with the word for 'time' and so 'death,' and who is regarded as the Destroyer; Durgā, which may be an aboriginal word, though it is generally taken to mean 'inaccessible,' either as a description of the goddess herself or because she is pictured as the slayer of a demon whom it was difficult to get at; Bhairavī, the terror-inspiring; Chaṇḍī, the fierce one; Pārvatī, the mountain goddess, daughter of Himālaya; Kumārī, the maiden; Umā, whose characteristics are gracious, and who may originally have been a mountain goddess, though a connection is also possible with *amma*, the

[1] *Brahmanism and Hinduism*, p. 187. The numbers 1,008, 108, 58, 38, 28, 18, 12, 10, 8 play an important part in the *Tantras*. Cp. Hauer, *Die Dhāraṇī*, p. 8. Dubois, *Hindu Manners*, p. 224, records that the string holding the gold ornament or *tali* worn by all married women is made of 108 fine threads.

common name for the mother-goddesses of the Dravidians; Gaurī, a goddess of harvest, who may have got her name from the ripe corn, or from the yellowish Gaura buffalo. Around these and the many other names numerous legends cluster.[1] They show how long and complicated has been the history of the sect.

Traces of Śākta worship occur almost all over India, though its greatest hold has been in Bengal and Assam. The Himālayas are regarded as the abode of Śiva and his wife; the mountain Gaurī-Śankara, which is near to, though not identical with, Everest, bears their names. The Cape at the southern end of the Indian peninsula has a temple to the virgin-goddess, and its name, Comorin, is said to be a corruption of Kumarī Devī. Sister Nivedita tells how the Swami Vivekānanda arrived there once too poor to pay for a ferry across to the shrine, and so was compelled to swim the shark-infested strait.[2] In the west, at Hinglāj, in Baluchistan, Pārvatī is worshipped by many pilgrims, and even by the local Muhammadans. Over 1,500 miles to the east is the Kāmagiri or Nilāchal hill in the old kingdom of Kāmarūpa, where stands one of the most holy of all the shrines. In Central India, near Mirzapur, is a temple where Kālī is worshipped under the name Vindhyācalavāsinī, 'dweller in the Vindhya mountains,' and this is one of the most important centres from the historical point of view. Kālī was also the tutelary goddess of Chitor in Rājputāna.

One of the chief legends of the cult, which seeks to explain the sanctity of the chief places of worship, is evidence of its widespread character. It is said that Satī, the wife of Śiva, died of sorrow because of the discourtesy shown to her husband by her father Daksha. Overcome by grief and remorse, Śiva wandered about the world, carrying his wife's dead body on his head as a penance. The other gods were afraid lest Śiva should by this means obtain excessive power, so Vishṇu pursued him, and with successive blows of his discus cut the body to bits. It fell to earth in fifty-one pieces, and around each there grew up a *pīṭhasthāna*, a sacred

[1] On some of the legends connected with Umā, Pārvatī, Gaurī, Durgā, etc., see Wilkins, *Hindu Mythology*.

[2] *The Master as I Saw Him*, p. 99 f.

place to which pilgrimages are made. Glasenapp has collected many of the details about these shrines in his *Heilige Stätten Indiens.* At Kāmagiri the generative organs (*yoni*) of Satī are said to have fallen,[1] at Hinglāj the top of her head. Kālighāt, near Calcutta, is probably today the most famous centre of Śākta worship, and there some of the toes, or, according to other accounts, a finger fell.[2] The tongue came down at Jvālāmukhī, in the Panjab; the temple lies over flames of burning gas, and these are worshipped instead of an image. At Jājpur, in Orissa, at Mount Girnar, in the Bombay Presidency (where the Aghoris, ascetics who despised everything earthly, and eat human flesh and excrement, used to assemble), at Kāngra, in the Panjab (whose famous Durgā temple was plundered by Mahmud of Ghazni in A.D. 1009), at Ujjain, capital of Mālwa and one of the seven sacred cities of India, and at Kāśī or Benares, another sacred city (Satī's ear-rings fell in the Maṇikarṇi pool there, where now stands the so-called 'Monkey Temple'), the goddess is worshipped. In spite of her dismemberment by Vishṇu, she was reborn as Umā, according to the legends, and is now identified also with Durgā and Kālī.

J. N. Bhattacharya, in his *Hindu Castes and Sects*, suggests that most of the Brāhmans in Bengal, Mithila and the Panjab are Śāktas of a moderate type.[3] How little or how much this can mean will be clearer when we have considered the divisions within the sect, and the relations to it of certain other groups. Hindu eclecticism makes such a study very difficult. As soon as the observance of the ancient sacrifices prescribed in the *Śrauta-sūtras* began to decline, we find orthodox twice-born men, known as *Smārtās*, worshipping the five gods, *pañcha deva*, Vishṇu, Śiva, Durgā, Sūrya and Gaṇeśa, in what is called *Pañchāyatana pūjā.* The same temple may contain shrines to all of these deities, the one in the centre being regarded as the special patron, or *iṣṭa-*

[1] Devendranath Tagore visited the temple of Kamakhya on the Nilāchal hill in 1849. In his *Autobiography*, Chap. XXV, he says: 'It is not a temple, but a cave in the rocks, in which there was no image, only a *yoni mudra.*' Eliot describes a visit in 1910.

[2] Cp. descriptions by Ward, III, p. 118 f.; and Valentine Chirol, *India, Old and New*, p. 9 f.

[3] Pp. 44, 48, 52.

ŚĀKTA WORSHIPPERS IN THE COURTYARD AT KALIGHAT

ŚĀKTA WOMEN AT KALIGHAT, PRAYING AT THE SACRED CACTUS-TREE FOR THE GIFT OF CHILDREN

devata.[1] A man may therefore worship Durgā without really identifying himself with the Śākta sect.

The Devī has, however, her own distinctive temples and shrines. The older ones were often built in or near the cremation-ground or *śmaśāna*, for there at dead of night certain of the more primitive and revolting rites were performed. Many of the Śākta ascetics lived in the graveyards, and Indian literature contains many memorable descriptions of their horrors, to some of which we shall have occasion later to refer. Weak mortals were held to do the goddess service by loving, begetting, slaying, because Nature appears to create only to destroy, to create only because she destroys. Life and Death seem to go hand in hand, the one but the shadow of the other.

It is certain that human sacrifice once played a large part in the cult. In the earlier literature there are many allusions. Bāṇabhaṭṭa, a Brāhman living at the court of King Harsha early in the seventh century A.D., even refers to the sale of human flesh.[2] During the same reign the Chinese pilgrim, Hiouen Tsang, narrowly escaped being sacrificed to Durgā by Ganges pirates, and was only saved by a sudden typhoon. In the sixteenth century the Muhammadans found the offering of human beings common in Bengal. William Ward, the Serampore missionary, who visited Kālighāt first in 1801, speaks of it as a thing of the past, but as late as 1824 Bishop Heber met people who had seen boys sacrificed at the gates of Calcutta, and the Abbé Dubois, whose work is a trustworthy authority on the state of India south of the Vindhya mountains between 1792 and 1823, speaks particularly of the sacrifice of girls.[3] Since 1835 the whole practice has been illegal, and it is now generally repudiated by Śāktas themselves, but to this day in parts of Assam, and even in Bengal and Rājputāna, there is danger of the more primitive peoples secretly maintaining the custom.

The 'Blood Chapter,' or *Rudhirādhyāya*, of the *Kālikā Purāṇa*, probably a fourteenth century document, may be

[1] On the Śrautas and Smārtas see Farquhar, *ORLI*.

[2] Cp. *Harsha-charita*, pp. 92 f., 136, 263.

[3] Cp. *Baptist Missions*, II, p. 220; Dubois, *Hindu Manners*; Gait, 'Human Sacrifice (Indian),' *ERE*, VI, p. 849 f.

taken as typical of the instructions which used to be given to the worshippers:

Birds, tortoises, alligators, fish, nine species of wild animals, buffaloes, bulls, he-goats, ichneumons, wild-boars, rhinoceros, antelopes, iguanas, reindeer, lions, tigers, men, and blood drawn from the offerer's own body, are looked upon as proper oblations to the goddess Chaṇḍikā. . . . By a human sacrifice, attended by the forms laid down, Devī is pleased 1,000 years, . . . and by the sacrifice of three men 100,000 years. . . . Let a human victim be sacrificed at a place of holy worship, or a cemetery where dead bodies are burnt. . . . The victim must be a person of good appearance, and be prepared by ablutions, and requisite ceremonies, such as eating consecrated food the day before, and by abstinence from flesh and venery; and must be adorned with chaplets of flowers and besmeared with sandal wood. . . . Let the sacrificer worship the victim. . . . When this is done, O my children! the victim is even as myself, . . . then Brahmā and all the other deities assemble in the victim, . . . and he gains the love of Mahādevī, . . . who is the goddess of the whole universe, the very universe itself. . . . Let not the female, whether quadruped or bird or woman be ever sacrificed; the sacrificer of either will undoubtedly fall into hell. . . . Let not a Brahman be sacrificed; nor a prince, . . . nor one who is unwilling. . . . Having first worshipped the victim, whether human, beast, or bird, as directed, let the sacrificer immolate him, uttering the *mantra* directed for the occasion, and address the Deity with the text laid out before. . . . Now listen to the good and bad omens, to be drawn from the falling of the head, when severed from the body. . . . A prince may sacrifice his enemy, having first invoked the axe by holy texts, by substituting a buffalo or goat, calling the victim by the name of the enemy, throughout the whole ceremony, . . . infusing by holy texts the soul of the enemy into the body of the victim, which will, when immolated, deprive the foe of his life also. . . .[1]

Terrible and revolting as are the details here given, it is to be noted that it is provided that no females be offered to the goddess, and that the victim, if human, be a willing one. Gilbert Murray has described 'the curious cruelty of early agricultural works, the human sacrifices, the scapegoats, the tearing in pieces of living animals, and perhaps of living men, the steeping of the fields in blood,' which occurred in Greece, and his words apply also to India: 'Like most cruelty it had its roots in terror, terror of the breach of tabu—the

[1] The translation is by W. C. Blaquire, and was originally published (1798) in *Asiatic Researches*, Vol. V. It was reprinted with notes by K. S. Macdonald in 1901.

Forbidden Thing. . . . But we have to remember that, like so many morbid growths of the human mind, it has its sublime side. We must not forget that the human victims were often volunteers.'[1]

Probably originally animal sacrifice was offered in all Hindu temples, but its popularity must have been affected by the wide acceptance of the doctrine of *ahiṁsā*, i.e. non-injury to living things, which the Buddhists stressed. In the *Bhagavadgītā*, which belongs probably to the first or second century A.D., vegetarian offerings are said to be pleasing to Kṛishṇa.[2] It appears that animal sacrifices became gradually rarer. They were surrendered first by the Vaishṇavas, then by the Śaivas, and today are scarcely found anywhere except in the temples of the goddess, and in a few Śaiva shrines dedicated to the more terrible forms of Śiva. It seems possible that no animal sacrifice was ever allowed in the *Pañchāyatana* temples.

Even among the Śāktas there have been those who have protested against bloodshed, and those who have tried to spiritualise the texts on which it is based. The best of the *Tantras* have always insisted that external worship alone is of no avail. 'If the mere rubbing of the body with mud and ashes gains liberation, then the village dogs who roll in them have attained it,' says the *Kulārṇava Tantra* (i), which is at least as old as the thirteenth century.[3] According to the *Mahānirvāṇa Tantra* (XIV, 115, 116, 122), an eighteenth century document, liberation 'does not come from the recitation of hymns, sacrifice, or a hundred fasts. Man is liberated by the knowledge that he is himself Brahman. . . . The state of mind in which it is realised that Brahman alone is is the highest; that on which there is meditation on the Brahman is the middle; praise and recitation of hymns is the next, and external worship is the lowest of all.'

[1] *Four Stages of Greek Religion*, pp. 48–49. The Greek rites are more closely paralleled by those of the aboriginal Konds, among whom human sacrifice was only suppressed with great difficulty. Buffaloes are now the victims.

[2] IX, 26.

[3] The *Kulārṇava T.* is given in the list of Lakshmīdhara, a scholar who lived at the end of the thirteenth century. Cp. *ORLI*, pp. 265, 268, etc.

These statements prepare us for the passionate protests of Rām Prasād, the great eighteenth century Śākta poet, whose attitude to sacrifices is like that of one of the Hebrew prophets of the eighth century B.C. to the savage cults of Canaan.

From all this pomp of worship the mind grows proud. Worship Kālī in secret that none may know. What is thy gain from images of metal, stone or earth? Fashion her image with the stuff of mind, and set it on the lotus-throne of your heart. Parched rice and plantains, ah! how vainly do you offer these! Feed her with the nectar of devotion, and satisfy your own mind. . . . Why do you bring sheep and goats and buffaloes for sacrifice? Saying, 'Victory to Kālī, Victory to Kālī,' sacrifice the six passions.

Prasād says: What need is there of drums and tom-toms? Saying, 'Victory to Kālī,' clap your hands and lay your mind at Her Feet.[1]

Woodroffe tells us that passages such as that quoted above from the 'Blood Chapter' have both a material (*sthūla*) and a subtle (*sūkshma*) meaning. Commenting on a hymn to Kālī, in which it is said that the goddess delights to receive in sacrifice the hair, flesh and bones of goat, buffalo, cat, sheep and camel, and also those of man, he writes:

In its literal sense this passage may be taken as an instance of man-sacrifice, of which we find traces throughout the world (and in some of the *Tantras*) in past stages of man's evolution. Nothing is more common in all religions (and Christianity, as by some understood, provides many examples) than to materially understand spiritual truths. . . . Even in the past the spiritual referred such sacrifice to the self; an inner sacrifice which all must make who would attain to that spirit which we may call Kālī, God, Allah, or what we will. But what is the *Svarūpa-vyākhyā*, or true meaning, of this apparently revolting verse. The meaning is that inner or mental worship is done to her who is black because she is the boundless consciousness whose true nature is eternal liberation. And just as in outer worship material offerings are made, so the *sādhaka* sacrifices to Her his lust (the Goat—*Kāma*), his anger (the Buffalo—*Krōdha*), his greed (the Cat—*Lōbha*), his stupidity of illusion (the Sheep—*Mōha*), his envy (the Camel—*Mātsaryya*) and his pride and infatuation with worldly things (the Man—*Mada*). All will readily recognise in these animals and man the qualities (*guṇa*) here attributed to them.[2]

[1] *BRLS*, No. XVIII. With the Six Passions (Lust, Anger, Greed, Stupidity of illusion, Pride and Envy) compare the Seven Deadly Sins of the Western Middle Ages.

[2] *SS*, p. 309. He is commenting on the *Karpūrādi Stotra*, XIX. The passage is typical of his style and method.

It is worth noting that Woodroffe does admit traces in some of the *Tantras* of actual human sacrifices. Does he mean that the spiritual man has always understood the language of sacrifice purely figuratively, or that the outward offering should be accompanied by an inward one? The attitude of a Rām Prasād to the darker side of the cult seems a much healthier and a more honest one than this allegorising suggested by Woodroffe. 'These attempts at covering up the marks of the old state of morality,' says Govinda Das, with the writings of some Indian apologists in mind, 'may do credit to the sensitive feeling and the patriotism of the allegorists; but they fail to convince.'[1] It is important, however, to realise, in view of the sweeping statements which have often been made, that such repudiations of the literal meaning of the texts come from Śāktas themselves.

The offering of one's own blood has always been common, particularly among women, and it continues to the present day. Writing in 1902, Murdoch quotes a learned Hindu as saying: 'There is scarcely a respectable house in Bengal the mistress of which has not at one time or other shed her own blood under the notion of satisfying the goddess by the operation.'[2] Hibiscus flowers have become a favourite present to Kālī, probably because they are the colour of blood.[3] Frequently the statue of the goddess is consulted as a kind of oracle; betel leaves are presented, and the worshipper draws his conclusions as to the will of the goddess from the way they rest or fall.

There are certain special festivals during the year, the most important in Bengal being the *Durgā-pūjā*, which occurs in late September or October.[4] The more terrifying aspects of the goddess are in the background. It is the time of

[1] *Hinduism*, p. 224. [2] *Śiva Bhakti*, p. 25.

[3] Woodroffe, *SS*, p. 115, suggests that the Hibiscus may have been introduced from China, via Nepal, and that we have here traces of Buddhist influence on the cult. Glasenapp, *Brahma und Buddha*, p. 152, accepts this.

[4] Cp. Jarl Charpentier, 'Meaning and Etymology of Pūjā,' *Indian Antiquary*, May and July, 1927; Glasenapp, op. cit., p. 133; P. Ghosha, *Origin of the Durgā Pūjā*.

family reunions, a happy festival comparable to the Western Christmas. According to the legends, Umā or Gaurī, the daughter of Himālaya and Menakā, was married to Śiva at the age of eight; at the time of the *pūjā* she is supposed to re-visit her parents, who have in the meantime discovered the grim character of their son-in-law, and whose hearts go out in sympathy to their child, now with them for a brief space. It is not difficult to imagine the appeal of such a story. The *Āgamanī* (advent) and *Vijayā* (victory) songs are used at this time. Specimens of these lyrics can be found in the pages of Rabindranath Tagore, and in the *Bengali Religious Lyrics: Śākta*, of Thompson and Spencer.

Now has the happy night ended in dawn (sings Rām Prasād), behold thy daughter comes. Go greet her entrance home again. Come, see her face beauteous as the moon! Your sorrows will all disappear. What stores of honey fall from the moonbeams that are her smiles. . . .

Happy indeed at heart is Rāmprasāda Dāsa the poet. He swims in a great sea of joy. At the advent of the Mother all men rejoice. So lost are they in happiness that day and night are both alike to them.[1]

The more genial side of Śāktism is in evidence at the *Durgā-pūjā*. Even before there was a vigorous Nationalist movement in Bengal, there were special patriotic celebrations at this time. It has been a kind of Christmas and Empire Day combined. Tagore, in a letter dated October 5th, 1894, and written from Calcutta, refers to the making of images in preparation for the *pūjā*.

Once every year there comes a period when all minds are in melting mood, fit for the springing of love and affection and sympathy. The songs of welcome and farewell to the goddess, the meeting of loved ones, the strains of the festive pipes, the limpid sky and molten gold of autumn, are all parts of one great pæan of joy. Pure joy is children's joy. They have the power of using any and every trivial thing to create their world of interest, and the ugliest doll is made beautiful with their imagination and lives with their life. He who can retain this faculty of enjoyment after he has grown up is indeed the true Idealist, . . . A whole people approaches nearest to this blissful state at such seasons of festivity. And then what may ordinarily appear to

[1] *BRLS*, No. XCIII. The selection contains fifteen examples of this kind of song. On Tagore see Edward Thompson, *Tagore, Poet and Dramatist*, pp. 30, 160.

be a mere toy loses its limitations and becomes glorified with an ideal radiance.[1]

Of the Greek celebrations which correspond in so many respects to the *Durgā-pūjā*, Gilbert Murray writes: 'If Religion is that which brings us into relation with the great world-forces, there is the very heart of life in this home-coming Bride of the underworld (i.e. Persephone), life with its broken hopes, its disaster, its new-found spiritual joy; life seen as Mother and Daughter, not a thing continuous and unchanging but shot through with parting and death, life as a great love or desire ever torn asunder and ever renewed.[2]

Other special days are set apart for ceremonies commemorating various of the deeds of the goddess. They differ very much from district to district. Many of them are conveniently set out and noted in Miss Underhill's *Hindu Religious Year*.

One of the features of the worship which has achieved notoriety and has been the cause of much of the general condemnation of the Śāktas, is the secret *Chakra-pūjā* (circle-worship). Whatever may have been its origin, it seems to have become a recognised part of the cult about the same time as the Śākta *Tantras* began to appear, that is, from about A.D. 600. 'An equal number of men and women who may belong to any caste or castes, and may be near relatives — husband, wife, mother, sister, brother—meet in secret, usually at night, and sit in a circle. The goddess may be represented by an image or a *yantra*, which is actually a drawing of the *pudendum muliebre* in the centre of a circle formed by nine *pudenda*. The liturgy consists of the repetition of *mantras*, the ritual in partaking of the five *tattvās*, i.e. elements, viz. wine, meat, fish, parched grain, and sexual intercourse.'[3] The *tattvās* are vulgarly called the five M. or *Ma-Kāras*, because

[1] *Glimpses of Bengal*, pp. 145–47. In another letter from Shelidah, October, 1891, he describes those 'returning home from distant fields of work for the poojah vacation.'

[2] *Four Stages of Greek Religion*, p. 95.

[3] *ORLI*, p. 203. Cp. Winternitz, *Die Tantras, usw*, p. 156; Glasenapp, *Der Hinduismus*, p. 79 f.; Das, *Hinduism*, p. 334 f. Foy, *Uber das indische Yoni-Symbol*, makes some interesting suggestions regarding the origin of the *yoni* representations, which are not necessarily always to be connected, in his opinion, with the *pudendum muliebre*.

each of the Sanskrit names begins with that letter: *Madya*, *Māṇsa*, *Matsya*, *Mudrā* and *Maithuna*.[1] Even the *Mahānirvāṇa Tantra*, a late eighteenth century work, which has been described as 'by far the greatest and best book belonging to the sect,' and which, according to Woodroffe, 'evidences what may be called a reforming tendency on account of abuses which had occurred,' contains regulations for this *Chakrapūjā*.[2]

The principle underlying the *Pañchatattva* worship appears to be that poison is the antidote of poison, and men must rise by those very things through which they so often lose their manhood. The *Kulārṇava Tantra* declares: 'As one falls on the ground one must lift oneself by aid of the ground.' The symbols chosen are very obvious ones; wine, the medicine, dispeller of care and source of merriment; flesh, nourisher of the body; fish, the tasty giver of generative power; corn from the earth, and finally sexual intercourse, speaking of the love and joy of creation. Obviously such rites are an encouragement to immorality, and could not long be tolerated by those of a healthily developed moral sense, but it is well that we consider their intention in the best possible light. The texts suggest far greater safeguards against unrestrained licence than Western critics have usually admitted. Even H. H. Wilson points out that, 'in justice to the doctrines of the sect, it is to be observed that these practices, if instituted merely for sensual gratification, are held to be as illicit and reprehensible as in any other branch of the Hindu faith.'[3] The texts make it clear that the worshippers must be pure in heart, free from desire and lust, and conscious that they are taking part in a sacrament, the aim of which is to unite participants with the *Śakti*, and to free them from the fetters of the ordinary man. It is only under certain conditions that

[1] In older works, e.g. Wilson, p. 164, *mudrā* was rendered 'mystic gestures,' but against this Avalon vigorously protests, and Farquhar, Winternitz, Glasenapp, etc., accept his correction. Sten Konow, however, in the new edition of Chantepie de la Saussaye, keeps to the older rendering and suggests it is an alternative for *madhu*, honey. He is here probably following Bhandarkar, *Vaishṇavism, Śaivism, etc.*, p. 147.

[2] Farquhar, *Modern Religious Movements*, p. 304; *SS*, p. 328.

[3] *Religious Sects*, p. 168.

there can be any other representative of *Śakti* for a man than his lawful wife. 'Generally speaking,' says Woodroffe, 'we may distinguish not only between Dakshināchāra and Vāmāchāra, in which the full rites with wine and Śakti are performed, but also a Vāma and Dakshina division of the latter Āchāra itself. It is only on the former side that there is worship with a woman other than the Sādhaka's own wife.'[1] If a man have no wife, or if she be 'incompetent,' that is, not on the same plane of development, then union with another *Śakti* is by many considered legitimate, but his relationship with her is then permanent in character. She becomes the devotee's wife 'in religion,' though the children of such a 'marriage' are not recognised as legitimate.[2]

None of these safeguards or explanations, however, alters the fact that this *chakra-pūjā* is one of the biggest blots on the sect. Woodroffe assures us that it is 'either disappearing or becoming in spirit transformed,'[3] which may be taken as a confession of the abuses to which it has led.

There has been much debate as to the relation of *pañcha-tattva* worship to the *Vedas*. The movement represented by Devendranath Tagore and the Brahma Samāj regarded the *Purāṇas* as 'a storehouse of mythological and historical legends,' and the *Tantras* as showing 'an esoteric phase of Hinduism,' and turned from them to the *Upanishads* and what was regarded as the lofty though simple worship of the *Vedas*.[4] Modern scholarship does not support quite this view. Woodroffe seems to be right when he urges that 'the present-day general prohibition against the use of wine, and the generally prevalent avoidance or limitation of an animal diet, are due to the influence of Jainism and Buddhism, which arose after, and in opposition to, Vedic usage. Their influence is most marked, of course, in Vaishṇavism, but has not been without effect elsewhere. When we examine ancient

[1] *SS*, p. 350. Cp. *Tantra of the Great Liberation*, Introduction, p. cxi f. Dakshināchāra = right hand, and Vāmāchāra = left hand. The terms are applied to divisions within the sect. See below Chap. III.

[2] *Mahānirvāṇa T.*, IX. Cp. C. S. Ranga Iyer, *Father India*, p. 52. 'A Devadasi who is in the keeping of one man does not go to another man.'

[3] *SS*, p. 61.

[4] *Autobiography*, pp. 102–3, 109, etc.

Vedic usage, we find that meat, fish and *mudrā* were consumed, and intoxicating liquor was drunk in Vedic *Yajñas*. We also discover some Vedic rites in which there was *maithuna*.'[1] The Śāktas have good ground for urging that in many of their rites they are reverting to, or continuing, the practices of their ancestors. Berriedale Keith's careful words are worth noting in this connection: 'It is impossible to understand Indian religion unless the sectarian standpoint and Śākta rites are understood; nothing is more erroneous than to regard them as essentially alien to Vedic religion; even so hieratic a text as the *Ṛigveda* reveals a defence of Indra against those who denied his divinity which points unmistakably to sectarian devotion, and the fertility magic of such rites as the Mahāvrata at the winter solstice, of the horse sacrifice and even of the Soma sacrifice, affords precedent for the ceremonies which repel us in the *Tantras*.'[2]

Two other phases of the cult require mention. The average Śākta seeks to acquire supernatural faculties with the help of the goddess, and enlists her aid for the destruction of his enemies. Sorcery is employed for white and black purposes. There is an elaborate *yoga* practice, the following of which, it is claimed, brings a man to perfection (*siddhi*). This *yoga* method depends partly on the analysis of the sacred syllable OM, of which certain *Upanishads* treat. Every letter of the alphabet is regarded as filled with *Śakti*, and from them mysterious one-syllable words (*bījas*) and longer spells (*mantras*) are constructed. Many of them are mere nonsense syllables, 'sparks,' as Farquhar has expressed it, 'from the blazing furnace of aboriginal superstitions whence the system arose, or from the equally superstitious stores laid up in the *Atharvaveda*.'[3] Rudolf Otto, in *The Idea of the Holy*, treats OM as an 'original numinous sound.' Many of these strange syllables seem to have been the product of the

[1] *SS*, p. 60 f. Cp. Appendix II, *The Vedas and the Tantras*, by B. L. Mukherji.

[2] *International Review of Missions*, IX, p. 609; cp. Monier Williams, *Brahmanism and Hinduism*, p. 196; Das, *Hinduism*, p. 124; Glasenapp, *Brahma u. Buddha*, p. 152. For the Mahāvrata sacrifice see J. W. Hauer, *Der Vrātya*, pp. 246–96; Keith, *Religion of the Vedas*, p. 351 f.

[3] *ORLI*, p. 201.

ŚĀKTA YANTRAS

(Symbolic Representations of Mystical Power)

(Reproduced from A. Avalon's *Hymns to the Goddess*, by kind permission of Messrs. Luzac & Co.)

ecstatic states induced by the *yoga* exercises, and can be paralleled from the phenomena of 'speaking with tongues' in many other parts of the world. The *mantras* are used as a protection against demons, for magical purposes, and for meditation. 'A *mantra*,' says Woodroffe, 'consists of certain letters arranged in definite sequence of sounds, of which the letters are the representative signs. To produce the desired effect, the *mantra* must be intoned in the proper way according to both sound (*varna*) and rhythm (*tvara*). For these reasons a *mantra* when translated ceases to be such, and becomes a mere word or sentence.'[1] In the first volume of *Tantrik Texts*, edited by Avalon, glossaries are published which give the Tāntric significance of various words and sounds. The whole idea of the *mantra* as employed in the Śākta system goes back to the conception of sound as an essential part of the supreme, something possessing supernatural value and potency. We know now enough of the laws of the mind to understand how such things can appeal to and affect the untutored and credulous. The popularity of *mantras* for various purposes among the Śāktas throws important light on their conception of God. In one of his scornful attacks on idolatry Tagore has the haunting line: 'Those whose insolence would endow Thee with life by their *mantras*—who will endow them with life?'[2]

Various gestures (*mudrās*) are thought to add to the potency of the *mantras* during their murmuring or repetition (*japa*). Here again we have something that can be paralleled in other religious systems. Something of the same mental attitude underlies even the making of the sign of the Cross in certain forms of Christianity. In Śākta worship *Yantras* are also used; that is, slabs, usually of metal or stone, with variously constructed designs upon them. Probably originally the *yantra* was simply a sacred stone marked with some distinctive symbol. Frequently the symbolic diagram now contains a *mantra*, and is used for the purposes of meditation. Examples can be found reproduced by Avalon on the covers of his books, and in Zimme's *Kunstform und Yoga*.

[1] *SS*, p. 229.
[2] Cp. Thompson, *Tagore, Poet and Dramatist*, p. 190.

The *yoga* practice is built up on what seems to a Westerner a phantastic physiology. The body is believed to contain an immense number of channels (*nāḍī*) of occult force, and six large circles (*chakra*) or lotuses (*padma*), 'vital centres within the spinal column in the white and grey matter,'[1] the lowest and most important of which contains Brahmā in the form of a *liṅga* and the Devī asleep, coiled three and a half times round the *liṅga* like a serpent. The goddess is then called Kuṇḍalinī, the coiled one, and it is the object of the devotee to awaken her and draw her up through the different circles by way of the spinal cord (*sushumṇā*), that he may enjoy divine bliss. The process is known as the piercing of the six *chakras* (*shaṭchakrabheda*). Eliot records that it is said to be painful and even dangerous to health, and that it is admittedly 'unintelligible without oral instruction from a Guru.' This he has not had, but he is of opinion that 'strange and fanciful as the descriptions of *Shaṭchakrabheda* may seem, they can hardly be pure inventions, but must have a real counterpart in nervous phenomena which apparently have not been studied by European physiologists and psychologists.'[2] This view is supported by the recent book by an Indian doctor, Vasant G. Rele, to which Woodroffe supplies an introduction, which is far more hesitant in regard to the whole subject than Avalon's introduction to *The Serpent Power*. In *The Mysterious Kundalini*, Rele argues that the basis of this *yoga* method is the right Vagus nerve, 'which supplies and controls all the important vital organs through different plexuses of the sympathetic portion of the autonomic system.'[3] Complicated and lengthy exercises appear to make it possible for the subject to gain considerable control of the nervous system and thus to regulate the functions of the body to an extent of which Westerners have little knowledge. Along these lines explanations may later be forthcoming of some of the miracles ascribed to the holy men of India, as well as of some of the claims to supernatural powers made by the Śāktas.

In the *Tantras* detailed instructions are given for the

[1] *SS*, p. 410. [2] *Hinduism and Buddhism*, I, p. 311.

[3] p. 57. The six centres are located between the root of the genitals and the anus (*mūlādhāra*), in the genitals (*svādisthāna*), abdomen (*manipūra*), heart (*anāhata*), throat (*vishuddha*) and eyes (*ājnā*).

attainment and exercise of magical powers. Woodroffe has some interesting remarks on magic, which show the line of defence adopted by modern apologists. After pointing out that magic is found in plenty in the *Atharvaveda*, he continues: 'There is nothing wrong in magic *per se*. As with so many other things, it is the use or abuse of it that makes it right or wrong. . . . Magic is likely to be abused and has in fact been abused by some Tantriks. I think this is the most serious fact established against them. For evil magic which proceeds from malevolence is a greater crime than any abuse of natural appetite.'[1] From what follows it is evident that Woodroffe believes that modern scientific investigation has established the objectivity of the leading phenomena of occultism, 'e.g. that Thought is itself a Force, and that by thought alone, properly directed, without any known physical means, the thought of another, and hence his whole condition, may be affected.'[2] Under the cloak of such beliefs many 'magical' practices have of late years been revived by the Śāktas.

[1] *SS*, p. 53. [2] *Ibid.*, p. 55 f.

CHAPTER III

THE GODDESS AND HER WORSHIPPERS

THE goddess is often represented in a manner repellent to Western eyes. It is intended that she should strike terror and create awe in the minds of her worshippers, and these feelings have not been wholly absent even from those who have regarded her with trust and affection. Rudolf Otto, in *The Idea of the Holy*, has drawn attention to the frequent union of elements of terror, awe and yet fascination in all levels of religious experience.[1]

The *Yoginī Tantra*, probably a sixteenth century work, speaks of

> her who is crane-like (i.e. white), with rows of teeth resplendent as the beauty of lightning, having the effulgence of a smooth new cloud sprung up in the rainy season, charming with rows of skull-necklaces, with flowing hair . . . with lolling tongue, with dreadful voice, with three eyes all red, having the circle of the mouth oozing (or glittering) with crores and crores of moons, . . . with two corpses as ear ornaments, bedecked with various gems, . . . girdled with thousands of dead men's hands, with smiling face, whose countenance is flecked with streams of blood dripping from the corners of her mouth, whose four arms are adorned with sword, severed heads, boons and security; with great teeth, . . . with blood-bedecked body, mounting upon the corpse of Śiva, . . . having her left foot set upon the corpse.[2]

An earlier but essentially similar description is to be found in the more famous *Chaṇḍīmāhātmya*, now a part of the *Mārkaṇḍeya Purāṇa*. Statues, reliefs and pictures of the god-

[1] Cp. in this connection Paul Tillich, *Das Dämonische, ein Beitrag zur Sinndeutung der Geschichte*, p. 8, on 'die übergreifende Form, die ein gestaltendes und gestaltzerstörendes Element in sich vereinigt, und damit ein Gegen-Positives, eine positive, d.h. formschaffende Formwidrigkeit.'

[2] Monro, *Macdonald MS*, p. 1. There are good reproductions in the works of Glasenapp, and in Mackenzie, *Indian Myth and Legend*.

dess reproduce these grotesque and disgusting features. The chorus of citizens in Tagore's play *Sacrifice* sings:

> The dread Mother dances naked in the battlefield,
> Her lolling tongue burns like a red flame of fire,
> Her dark tresses fly in the sky, sweeping away sun and stars,
> Red streams of blood run from her cloud-black limbs,
> And the world trembles and cracks under her tread.

It is now customary, in certain circles, to interpret such representations symbolically, and to find in them much hidden meaning. How this is done may be judged from the following sentences by Woodroffe:

> Kālī is set in such a scene (i.e. in the cremation ground) for she is that aspect of the Great Power which withdraws all things unto Herself at, and by, the dissolution of the Universe. He alone worships without fear who has abandoned all worldly desires and seeks union with Her as the one Blissful and Perfect Experience. On the burning ground all worldly desires are burnt away. She is naked and dark like a threatening rain-cloud. She is dark, for she is Herself beyond mind and speech, reduces all things into that worldly 'nothingness,' which, as the void of all that we now know, is at the same time the All which is Peace. She is naked, being clothed in space alone, because the great power is unlimited; further she is herself beyond *Māyā*: that Power of Hers which creates all universes. She stands upon the white corpse-like body of Śiva. He is white because he is the illuminating transcendental aspect of consciousness. He is inert because he is the changeless aspect of the Supreme, and she the apparently changing aspect of the same. In truth She and He are one and the same, being twin aspects of the One who is changeless in, and exists as, change.[1]

All this means little more than that it is now felt necessary to have some ideal explanation of the more repulsive features in the descriptions of the goddess. The modern worshipper seeks reasons and excuses for what must almost instinctively offend, except among more primitive peoples. This rationalising method, however, can in different hands yield very

[1] *SS*, p. 257 f.: 'The question before us is, what does this imagery mean now, and what has it meant for centuries past to the initiate in Her symbolism. . . . Does every Hindu worshipper think such profundities when he sees the figure of Mother Kālī? Of course not, no more than (say) an ordinary Italian peasant knows of or can understand the subtleties of either the Catholic mystics or doctors of theology.'

different results. Miss Underhill tells us that the story of Kālī's dancing upon Śiva is often explained as the tumult of human emotions which precedes the awakening of the human soul to the realisation of its origin from God. Suddenly man realises the truth of things, and stands aghast and shamed, like Kālī with outstretched tongue.[1] On the other hand, B. C. Bhattacharya asserts that the wild dance symbolises the darkness which enveloped the universe at the time of creation.[2] The allegorical method of exegesis leads always to various contradictory interpretations.

Some Śāktas are much more literal in their following of the sacred texts than others. There are many variations and differences of emphasis. Much has been written regarding divisions within the sect, and separate schools and traditions have been alleged to exist. Arthur Avalon is probably right in saying that 'their existence and nature have yet to be established,'[3] but he would agree that a broad distinction may be drawn between Right-hand Śāktas (*Dakshināchārīs*) and Left-hand Śāktas (*Vāmāchārīs*). This division is made by almost all European writers about the sect, though there seems often to have been misunderstanding as to its significance in the eyes of Śāktas themselves. The term 'left-hand,' when used by worshippers of the goddess, is not one of abuse, as many seem to have supposed. Nor are these names used after the manner of Martin Luther, who, attacking both the life of the world and the life of the cloister, described the one as *dextralis impius* and the other as *sinistralis impius*.[4] According to most modern Śākta apologists, the *Dakshināchāra* and the *Vāmāchāra* are both recognised forms of worship presented by the *Tantras* for different grades of worshippers. The authority for both is the same, but Left-hand Śāktas have advanced further towards the goal of complete union with the goddess. Great secrecy is maintained regarding the practices of the *Vāmāchārīs*, and undoubtedly to this day their worship involves and indeed encourages much that is repulsive and obscene, judged by modern standards, and much

[1] *Hindu Religious Year*, p. 106. [2] *Indian Images*, Pt. I, p. 41.
[3] *Principles of Tantra*, Pt. I, Preface, p. xiv.
[4] Cp. Heim, *Das Wesen des evangelischen Christentums*, p. 81.

that is condemned by other Hindus. Even Avalon admits 'the decadence of many of the followers of the *Vāmāchāra* community'[1] during last century.

The *Dakshināchārīs*, on the other hand, are, in many respects, scarcely distinguishable from other Hindus. Barth, in his *Religions of India*, states that a member of this branch of the Śāktas, 'except in insistence on animal sacrifice in honour of Durgā, Kālī, or other terrible forms of the goddess, observes the general usages of Hinduism.'[2] According to Monier Williams, there are 'some educated Hindus whose worship of this goddess amounts to little more than reverence for a personification of the energy of Nature.'[3] Crooke, with Bengal in mind, writes: 'To be a Śākta is very often merely to be an eater of meat and a drinker of spirituous liquor, both being permitted luxuries.'[4]

There seems no evidence in the early literature for a Devī-worshipping sect of such mild characteristics as the *Dakshināchārā* exhibits, and there has been considerable speculation as to the origin of this manner of worship. Probably it was connected with the gradual giving up of human sacrifice, and later of animal sacrifice. There is a tradition which connects the giving up of human sacrifice at Devī's temple in Conjeeveram (Kāñchipuram) with the great Hindu philosopher and controversialist, Śaṅkarāchārya, who lived at the end of the eighth century, and who had certainly close relations with the Śāktas, though he cannot be regarded as a Śākta in the sectarian sense. Slowly a reformed type of Devī worship spread. Later, the more advanced and enthusiastic devotees taught that this branch of the sect was but the first stage on the path to ecstasy (*samadhi*) and union with the divine. This is the attitude of the modern apologist, though it is certainly historically incorrect.

On the basis of two *Tantras*, the *Kulārṇava*, which is earlier than the thirteenth century, and the *Jñāndipa*, Woodroffe describes the various stages (*āchāras*) through which the

[1] *Principles of Tantra*, Pt. I, Introduction, p. viii.

[2] op. cit., p. 102. Cp. Farquhar, *Modern Religious Movements*, p. 303; Woodroffe, *SS*, p. 60.

[3] *Brahmanism and Hinduism*, p. 180.

[4] 'Bengal,' *ERE*, II, 490.

Śākta devotee seeks to pass.[1] They are usually traversed in a multitude of births, we are told, but 'the wearing of the spiritual garment is recommenced where it was dropped at the previous death.' According to the Sāṅkhya philosophy, with which, as we shall see, Śākta thought has, at certain points, close affinity, the evolution and diversity of the world are explained by the varied combination of three different substances or constituents (*guṇas*): *sattva*, *rajas* and *tamas*. These terms are very difficult to translate. *Sattva* stands for goodness, truth and reality, and is associated with the feeling of joy; *rajas*, distinguished by activity, corresponds to the passionate element in things; *tamas* is best rendered by darkness, obstruction or sloth. According to the *Tantras* which Woodroffe quotes, men may be divided into three classes:

1. *Paśus*. Those akin to animals, in whom *tamas* predominates.
2. *Vīras*. Heroes, in whom *rajas* is the chief quality.
3. *Divyas*. Divine beings, in whom *sattva* is dominant.

The worshipper (*sādhaka*) aims at reaching the highest of these classes, and seeks to become more and more free from the process of life and death and transmigration (*saṁsāra*), attached to nothing, hating nothing and ashamed of nothing. It is a long and costly procedure. Max Müller records the following saying of Rāmakṛishṇa: 'Two persons, it is said, began together the rite of invoking the goddess Kālī by the terrible process called *śavasādhanā* (a Tāntric invocation performed at night in the cemetery yard, the worshipper sitting on the body of a corpse). One invoker was frightened to insanity by the horrors of the earlier portion of the night; the other was favoured by the vision of the Divine Mother at the end of the night. Then he asked her, "Mother! why did the other man become mad?" The Deity answered, "Thou, too, O child! didst become mad many times in thy various previous births, and now at last thou seest me." '[2]

If a man is a Paśu, in order to become a Vīra he must

[1] *SS*, p. 78 f. Cp. *TGL*, Introduction, p. lxxviii f. This account of the stages of the way to salvation is reproduced by Sten Konow in the *Lehrbuch der Religionsgeschichte*, II, p. 179.

[2] *Life and Sayings of Ramakrishna*, No. 387, p. 185.

follow what may be generally termed the *Dakshināchāra*, but what is more correctly described as four stages:

A. 1. Veda. The *sādhaka* must carry out the prescriptions of the *Veda*. Fish and meat should not be eaten on certain days. Cohabitation with one's wife must be carefully regulated. The worship is largely of an external character. This has been described as the Path of Action (*kriyāmārga*). It is admitted that many of the Vedic rites cannot now be performed, and even a *Paśu* must therefore attend to the Āgamic ritual in this Kali age.[1]

2. Vaishṇava. The injunctions of the *Veda* are still followed but Vishṇu is worshipped. It is distinguished from the earlier stage by the endurance of great austerities (*tapas*), and by the contemplation of the Supreme everywhere. It is the Path of Devotion (*bhaktimārga*). The worshipper passes from a blind faith to an understanding of the supreme protecting energy of the Brahman.

3. Śaiva. Meditation is now on Śiva. This is the militant (*kshatrīya*) stage. To love and mercy are added strenuous effort and the cultivation of power. Entrance is made on the Path of Knowledge (*jñānamārga*).

4. Dakshina. This is the final preparation for passing out of the *Paśu* state. Meditation is on the *Devī*. Certain rituals are performed at night. Magic power (*siddhi*) is obtained by the use of a rosary of human bone. If *Pañchatattva* worship takes place, it is only performed with substitutes for the five elements.

B. 5. Vāma. Details of this path are kept secret because revelation destroys the *siddhi* attained thereby. The help of a spiritual director (*guru*) is throughout necessary. Passion, which has hitherto run 'downwards and outwards,' is now directed 'upwards and inwards,' and transformed into power. The bands which make a man a *Paśu* have gradually to be cut

[1] The *Āgamas* are manuals of religious practice dating from the eighth century onwards. Cp. Farquhar, *ORLI*, p. 190. According to Hindu chronology, we are living in the Kali age (*yuga*), hastening to utter destruction.

away; for example, pity, ignorance, fear, shame family convention, caste. There is worship with the *Pañchatattva* at night.

6. Siddhānta. This is superior to the previous stage, because the *sādhaka* shows knowledge, freedom from fear of the *Paśu*, adherence to the truth, and performs *Pañchatattva* worship openly.[1]

7 and 8. Aghora and Yoga. These are not always made into separate paths. The Aghorīs were ascetics who despised everything earthly, and ate human flesh and excrement.[2]

C. 9. Kaula. One can now become a *Divya*. Knowledge of this path unites one with Devī and Śiva. Every *dharma* is lost in the greatness of *Kuladharma*. There are no injunctions, no prohibitions, no restrictions as to time and place, no rules at all. One is beyond good and evil, and may indulge in practices which the general body of Hindus regard as unlawful. This is the 'do as you will' (*svecchāchāra*) stage. 'At heart a Śākta, outwardly a Śaiva, in gatherings a Vaishṇava, in thus many a guise the Kaulas wander on earth.' The Kaula or Kulina is one who 'sees the imperishable and all-pervading self in all things, and all things in the self.'

This elaborate plan of salvation can only gradually have been formulated. Its aim is completeness, and the defining of the orthodox Śākta attitude to the other great Hindu sects. These are accepted as necessary stages to something higher. The change from one mode of discipline and worship to another is commoner in India than in the West. The Methodist missionary, Dr. E. Stanley Jones, has recently told of a Hindu, who, speaking of his quest for God, remarked: 'I started in at Vishṇuism, then I went to Brahmoism, now I am in Śāktism, but I find myself relapsing into Vedāntism.'[3] It is to be noted in regard to the above scheme that a man may be born at any stage in the ascent, and that he himself, with

[1] Woodroffe, *SS*, p. 354, mentions Siddha Viras who were allowed special liberties with women.

[2] On the Aghorīs see Glasenapp, *HSI*, p. 153, and Plates 61–63.

[3] *Christ at the Round Table*, p. 29.

the assistance in the earlier *āchāras* of a *guru*, decides the point he has reached.

It is evident from this classification, and from other references by Woodroffe, that when the terms are carefully used there is a distinction between Vāmāchārīs and Kaulas. This has not always been recognised by European writers, though over thirty years ago it was insisted on by J. N. Bhattacharya in his *Hindu Castes and Sects.* The Kowls (*sic*) are there treated as a third main branch of the Śāktas, and the most extreme in their practices.[1] It is only after a *sādhaka* has fulfilled all the preceding *dharmas* that he is qualified for this *āchāra*, according to the theologians. There may have been different well-defined groups among the Kaulas. Arthur Avalon, in the introduction to one of the Tantric texts he has edited, writes:

> The *Kaulopanishad* is as it were the seed of the Kaula doctrine and form of worship, which is amplified in the *Kulārṇava* and other *Tantras* and *Saṁhitās*. There appear to have been different forms of Kaula worship, as evidenced by the commentary of Lakshṁīdhara on the *Saundaryalaharī*, who was himself a Kaula and a man of great learning, but spoke with severe condemnation of some of the practices of what he calls the Uttara or Northern Kaulas. . . . Towards the end of the Upanishad is to be found the injunction against the indiscriminate preaching of Kaula (Kula faith and doctrine). . . . This is because it is likely to be, as it is often in fact, misunderstood, as by persons who say that the doctrine teaches and sanctions, among other things, incest.[2]

Eggeling, writing in the *Encyclopædia Britannica*, speaks of the customs of the Kaulas as 'probably the most degrading cult ever practised under the pretext of religious worship.'[3] The Kaula, however, is a law unto himself, and it is hardly possible to speak of a cult in this connection. The only Prākṛit drama extant, the *Karpūramañjarī* of Rājaśekhara, who lived about A.D. 900 in the Western Deccan, contains a caricature of a Kaula magician, which throws light not only on the way such men were popularly regarded, but also on

[1] op. cit., pp. 407–13.

[2] *TT*, Vol. XI, Introduction, pp. 4–5. The extraordinary style is typical. Bhandarkar, *Vaishṇavism, Śaivism, etc.*, p. 147, notes a distinction between Purva (ancient) and Uttara (modern) Kaulas.

[3] *Ency. Brit.*, XIII, p. 511.

some of their practices. One of the songs of the magician is translated in lively fashion by C. R. Lanman:

BHĀIRAVĀNANDA (as if a little boozy)

As for black-book and spell,—they may all go to hell!
My teacher's excused me from practice for trance.
With drink and with women we fare mighty well,
As on—to salvation—we merrily dance!

A fiery young wench to the altar I've led.
Good meat I consume, and I guzzle strong drink;
And it all comes as alms,—with a pelt for my bed.
What better religion could anyone think?

Gods Vishṇu and Brahm and the others may preach
Of salvation by trance, holy rites, and the Vedies.
'Twas Umā's fond lover alone that could teach
Us salvation plus brandy plus fun with the ladies.[1]

A more literal rendering makes the allusions to Kaula teaching in this song even more definite. 'I know nothing of spells and Tantras. . . . Unto salvation we go, following the Kula way. . . . A hot strumpet has been consecrated as lawful wife. . . . To whom does the Kaula religion not appear charming?' This picture, even though it be a caricature, is a useful corrective to the laboured explanations of the theories behind the more extreme Śākta teaching, to which reference was made in the previous chapter.

There are other groups which have been associated more or less closely with the Śāktas. In *Mālatīmādhava*, the great Sanskrit drama of the eighth century, Aghoraṇṭa, the priest of the shrine of Chāmuṇḍā (one of the names of the goddess) is described as a Kāpālika ascetic. Already in the *Mahābhārata* the goddess is frequently given the epithet Kāpālī, wearer of skulls. Bankim Chatterji, the nineteenth century Bengali novelist, in *Kapālakuṇḍalā*, a story of the time of Akbar, refers to the devotee of the goddess from whom Nabakumar so narrowly escapes as the Kapalik. The word means 'skullman,' and seems to have been applied to an order of Śaiva ascetics, not easily distinguishable from the Kālāmukhas. They appear to have existed from the sixth

[1] Konow and Lanman, *Karpūramañjarī*, I, 22–24.

century onwards, and many of them worshipped the goddess with human sacrifice. References have already been made to the Aghorīs, another order of ascetics.[1]

The Thugs worshipped Kālī, and regarded their victims as sacrificed to her. Rabindranath Tagore has said of them: 'Their goddess frankly represented the principle of destruction. It was the criminal tribe's own murderous instinct deified—the instinct not of one individual, but of the whole community, and therefore held sacred.'[2] They can hardly be regarded as Śāktas in the full sense. Hopkins makes the interesting suggestion that they originated as a protest against the shedding of blood. Their victims were always throttled. Among several of the wild tribes whose divinities have been associated with Śiva's consort, there is found a definite refusal to bleed human victims. H. H. Wilson, in his work on the *Religious Sects of the Hindus*, refers to the practice in some cases of pummelling a sacrificial animal to death with the fists.[3] It is possible, then, as Hopkins suggests, that Thuggery may have been practised originally by 'an old conservative party, who wished to keep up the traditional throttling; though this is pure speculation, for, at the time when the sect became exposed, this means of death was merely the safest way to kill.'[4] The earliest reference to the Thugs comes from the middle of the twelfth century, and the first historical information from the end of the thirteenth. They owed part of their long immunity from attack to the religious basis of their actions. The temple of Kālī near Mirzapur, probably one of the oldest in existence, and still of considerable importance, was a centre to which the Thugs made pilgrimages. Although they were recruited originally from among the criminal tribes, in the nineteenth century they included many from the higher ranks of society.

[1] On the ascetics see Farquhar, *ORLI*, pp. 192, 211, 347, etc., and *The Fighting Ascetics of India* (John Rylands Library); Grierson, 'Kararis,' *ERE*, VII, p. 673; Das, *Hinduism*, p. 269 f.

[2] *Creative Unity*, p. 149: 'In the same manner, in modern churches, selfishness, hatred and vanity, in their collective aspect of national instincts, do not scruple to share the homage paid to God.'

[3] op. cit., p. 161.

[4] *Religions of India*, p. 493.

During the years 1831–37 they were systematically suppressed by the British Government.[1]

In *Bengali Religious Lyrics: Śākta*, the little book of translations issued by Edward Thompson and A. M. Spencer, a few poems by Baul singers are included. The Bauls were mendicant religious poets. They claimed to have been founded by Chaitanya, the great Vaishṇava revivalist of the early sixteenth century, but they were almost certainly earlier in origin, and possibly represent a fusion of Vaishṇavism with the already existing Śāktism, a fusion which in individual Bauls rises to something better than its constituents. Certainly many of their songs are Śākta in sentiment. Several Baul poems have been translated and praised by Rabindranath Tagore, and may be found scattered among his writings. Some lines from a modern song by one of these anonymous singers will serve to remind us that, in spite of the complicated divisions and rules, and the many loathsome practices historically associated with Śāktism, fine types of genuine piety have been produced. There are in this poem echoes of the protests of Rām Prasād against external sacrifices, but the author has an even wider tenderness and sympathy.

> You may give your sun-dried rice, you may give your sweetmeats, but do not think that with these you can gratify the Mother.
> Light the lamp of knowledge, offer the incense of an earnest soul; then only will one who is divine fulfil all your desires. Wild buffaloes and goats, these are the Mother's children; she does not want them as a sacrifice.
> If you would offer sacrifice, then slay your selfishness, and lay your love of ease upon the altar.
> Kāñgāl in anguish says: Where men make caste distinct from caste there can be no *śākti* worship. Let all the castes be as one and call to her as Mother, else will the Mother never grant us mercy.[2]

[1] Cp. Farquhar, 'Thugs,' *ERE*, XII, p. 259. Monier Williams was at Mirzapur in 1884. See *Brāhmanism and Hinduism*, pp. 575.

[2] *BRLS*, No. LXXXVIII.

CHAPTER IV

THE GROWTH OF ŚĀKTA IDEAS IN HINDU LITERATURE

THE earliest hymns of the *Ṛigveda* are the expression of the comparatively simple pastoral worship of the Aryan invaders of India. They are dated by most European scholars between 1500 and 1000 B.C., but it may well be that Indians are right in claiming for them a much greater antiquity.[1] Clearly centuries of religious development lie behind them. The gods are regarded for the most part as kindly, and are in the main personifications of the objects of Nature. 'The religion is a healthy, happy system. Neither asceticism nor austerity, neither pessimism nor philosophy, disturbs the sunshine of that early day.'

For our present purpose the most important point to be noticed is the very subordinate place assigned to goddesses in belief and worship. When they do appear they are vague and shadowy, very different from the chief figures, the vivid and genial Indra, or Varuṇa with his moral grandeur. They play hardly any part as rulers of the world. The most important is Ushas, goddess of dawn, the most poetically beautiful creation of the Ṛigvedic hymns.

> In the sky's framework she has shone with splendour;
> The goddess has cast off the robe of darkness.
> Wakening up the world with ruddy horses,
> Upon her well-yoked chariot Dawn is coming.[2]

Macdonnell is of opinion that her charm is 'unsurpassed in

[1] Cp. Glasenapp *Brahma und Buddha*, p. 50. 'Sicher ist es wohl, dass sie aus der Zeit vor 1500 v. Chr. stammen, wahrscheinlich, dass sie noch viel weiter zurückreichen, vielleicht bis in das 3. oder 4. Jahrtausend vor Beginn unserer Zeitrechnung.'

[2] *Ṛigveda*, I, 113. Translation by Macdonell.

the descriptive religious lyrics of any other literature.'[1] In the tenth book of the *Ṛigveda*, however, which on grounds of content and language is placed later than the others, Ushas seems to be losing her hold on the imagination of the singers. Instead, the Waters are praised as goddesses in four hymns, and Saraśvatī appears as a river goddess with three hymns to herself. At the end of his book *Shakti and Shakta*, Woodroffe prints an appendix on the *Vedas* and the *Tantras* by B. L. Mukherji, in which an attempt is made to find Vedic authority for the current conceptions of Durgā and Kālī. It is argued that Saraśvatī was one of the principal deities, and that by combining various references to her 'we have the almost complete form of a Devī, who is called at the present day by the name of Kālī.'[2] No attention is paid, however, to the various strata in the *Veda*, and the identifications are forced and unconvincing.

The earth-goddess, Prithivī (the Broad One) is hardly separated from her husband, Dyaus, the sky, the oldest of the gods, but one whose personification never got beyond a rudimentary stage. She is celebrated alone in only one short hymn of three stanzas (V, 84), and is certainly not conceived as a Great Mother in the Egyptian or early European sense, although six hymns celebrate Prithivī and Dyaus as universal parents. The *Atharvaveda* contains a long and beautiful hymn addressed to the Earth-goddess;[3] her husband is there, however not Dyaus but Parjanya, who seems to represent the rain-cloud. Throughout the hymn the poet never loses sight of material things. Prithivī's mystical and religious aspects interest him little. The *Atharvaveda* is a later collection of hymns than the *Ṛigveda*. It probably existed in its present form by 600 B.C., but it certainly contains much primitive Aryan animism as well as contributions from the religious lore of the conquered peoples. There is much in it that presents parallels to the magical instructions given in some of the *Tantras*.

Several of the Vedic gods are represented as having wives, but they are without independent character, and hardly

[1] *History of Sanskrit Literature*, p. 81.

[2] *SS*, p. 446. [3] XII, 1.

anything is known of them except their names, and these are in many cases formed simply by the addition of a feminine suffix to that of the god, e.g. Indrāṇī, Varuṇānī, Agnāyī.[1]

The *Brāhmaṇas* are usually assigned to the sixth, seventh and eighth centuries B.C., and represent the reflections of an age in which religion was in decay, and the priests claimed greater power than the gods themselves. The wives of the gods, occasionally mentioned in the *Ṛigveda*, have an established place in the cult apart from their husbands, but they are still vaguely conceived. So vast and varied became the mass of information which the worshipper must master that a new method of teaching was invented by the priests, that of the *Sūtras* or threads, 'long series of very abbreviated phrases, which served as a sort of classified index of the particular subject dealt with,'[2] and which the student was expected to commit to memory. It is in these *Sūtras* that the name of Rudrāṇī, the wife of Rudra, first appears, and she at once plays a more important part in the worship than any other goddess whose name is formed in a similar way.

Rudra was the prototype of Śiva. In the *Ṛigveda* he is one of the several deities identified with Agni, and is the chief of the Maruts, or storm gods, who accompany Indra. Although fierce and destructive, he can avert anger and evil, and can heal, if he so desire. There continues much controversy as to Rudra's origin. Weber has suggested that he represented the howling of the storm, and that, since the roaring of fire is similar, storm and fire combined to form a god of rage and destruction. Others connect him with the lightning. Oldenberg thinks he originally was a god of the mountain and forest, whence shafts of disease attack mankind. More recently, certain German scholars have suggested that Rudra was at first a god of the dead, or indeed the Vedic Death-god. The question cannot at present be settled. The various suggestions are important, however, because the character-

[1] For this and the following paragraphs see Macdonell, 'Vedic Mythology,' *G.I.P.A.*; and A. B. Keith, *Religion and Philosophy of the Veda*.

[2] *ORLI*, p. 38.

istics of Rudra Śiva are very similar to those later ascribed to the Devī.[1]

Buddhism has been described by a Hindu writer as 'a protestant reformation against the tyranny of birth and of bloody sacrifices.'[2] The centuries which followed its rise and spread are confused ones in the secular and religious history of India, particularly with regard to the developments within Hinduism. Already when the Buddha (*c.* 563–483 B.C.) was preaching, the educated Aryan mind was gravitating towards the philosophic and impersonal. The earliest *Upanishads* had been written, treatises on the mysterious and esoteric, which were the product of the mixture of Aryan and Dravidian thought, a mixture which, as A. B. Keith has urged, was like a chemical fusion, transforming both elements.[3] There are hints of monotheistic and pantheistic speculation in the later hymns of the *Ṛigveda*, in one of which occurs the often-quoted line: 'The one being priests speak of in many ways; they call it Agni, Yama, Mātariśvan' (I, 164). Thought about the origin of the Universe increased. *Brahman*, which may originally have meant prayer or magic and then came to stand for the sacred knowledge of the *Vedas*, without which no sacrifice could be valid, was finally used to express the essence of the Universe, the creative principle, the one Absolute Being. The *Upanishads* teach identity of this cosmic principle with the psychic principle, the *ātman* or self. Their message is that in the realisation of this identity lies salvation from re-birth (*saṁsāra*) and the law of *karma*. These two doctrines form the background of the *Upanishads*. Exactly when they arose it is impossible to say. There are only the vaguest hints of them in the earlier Vedic hymns, and Dravidian beliefs seem to have played a part in their development.[4] They had clearly a firm place in the popular imagination before the Buddhist era.

This elaboration of religious and philosophic thought can

[1] See Muir, *OST*, IV, 395 f., for translations of the relevant passages from Weber, *Indische Studien*, II, and Oldenberg. E. Arbman and H. Guntert connect Rudra with Death.

[2] Govinda Das, *Hinduism*, p. 50.

[3] *Religion and Philosophy of the Vedas*, p. 497.

[4] Cp. Glasenapp, *Brahma und Buddha*, pp. 41, 93.

have made little appeal to the average man. Nor did the teaching of the Buddha permanently meet men's need.[1] The great 'Protestant' faiths of Mahāvīra, the founder of Jainism, and Gautama, the Buddha, had neither of them rituals which the common people could substitute for the sacrifices and rites of the *Veda*. Gradually a complete transformation took place within both Hinduism and Buddhism. It was the period of the growth of the great Indian epics, the *Rāmāyaṇa* and the *Mahābhārata*. By the third or fourth centuries A.D., when these were complete, we find Śiva and Vishṇu as the chief gods, and even regarded as alternative forms of the one supreme personal god. The idea of personal union with the Supreme, instead of impersonal absorption, is taught. The doctrine of divine incarnation makes its appearance; there have been various descents to earth (*avatāras*) by the most important deities.

It is in the *Mahābhārata*, in portions which are probably late, but which supply evidence for the beliefs of an earlier period, that we find the first unmistakable signs of a sect whose worship centred in a goddess. The language in which she is addressed shows that a complete revolution had taken place in regard to female deities. In the preceding centuries many forces had been at work changing men's religious outlook. Gross animistic ideas must always have existed, side by side with much loftier beliefs, in the minds of the Aryan peoples; the conquered played an important part in modifying the faith and practice of their masters; it is known that there were fresh invasions into India from Central Asia, and the religion and culture of the newcomers no doubt made some contribution to the common stock; the significance of some of these things will be considered in greater detail in a later chapter. From the literature which has survived we note the striking change which took place.

In some of the *Upanishads*, which it is difficult to date very precisely, there are hints of a developing interest in female deities. Each of the great gods has his female counterpart. To Vishṇu there corresponds Vaishṇavī or Lakshmī; to Brahmā, Brahmāṇī or Sarasvatī; to Kārttikeya, god of war, Kārttikeyī;

[1] Cp. Govinda Das, *Hinduism*, p. 264.

to Indra, Indrāṇī; to Yama, Yamī; to Varāha, Varāhī; and to Śiva, Devī or Īśanī. As has already been noted, many of the names are formed by the mere addition of a feminine suffix to that of the god. In some places the separate cult of Lakshmī, the goddess of good-fortune, established itself, but, generally speaking, it was only the worship of Devī that became important. She took to herself the characteristics, attributes and even names of the others. The consort of Śiva became supreme, greater even than her husband, Maheśvara, himself. Several goddesses had by the end of the Vedic period come to be identified with the wife of Rudra-Śiva. Ambikā, who in the *Vājasaneyi Saṁhitā* (III, 5) is called his sister, in the *Taittirīya Āraṇyaka* (X, 18) is his spouse, and in the same work he is invoked as Umāpati. The names Durgā, Kātyāyanī, Kanyakumārī, Karālī, later regularly connected with the Devī, are found.[1]

An often-quoted but difficult passage occurs in the *Kena* (*Talavakāra*) *Upanishad*, in the third section, where it is related how on one occasion Brahmā gained a victory for the gods.[2] They, however, were inclined to take credit for themselves, so Brahmā appeared to disabuse them. He was not recognised until the resplendent Umā Haimavatī revealed his identity to Indra, and counselled the gods to rejoice in the victory of Brahmā. Umā has here been understood as a personification of knowledge (*vidyā*), but Sanskrit scholars feel that the epithet Haimavatī creates difficulties in the way of this interpretation, and, until we have a clearer understanding of the development of thought during this period, it seems impossible to explain how a goddess came to be regarded as a mediator between Brahmā and the other deities.

It is only in the *Mahābhārata*, in Yudhishṭhira's hymn to Durgā, and in that of Arjuna to the same goddess, that we find ourselves on firm ground. In the first hymn (IV. vi) Durgā is celebrated as the slayer of Mahisha, a demon-buffalo, and as a virgin goddess, whose constant abode is the Vindhya mountains. A doubtful reference may connect her with Kṛishṇa. There is in the second hymn (VI. xxiii) definite

[1] *Taittirīya Āraṇyaka*, X; *Muṇḍaka Upanishad*, I, 2, 4, etc.

[2] The passage is given in Muir, *OST*, IV, p. 420 f., with notes by Weber.

allusion to a legend linking the goddess with Kṛishṇa. At the same time she is more clearly identified with the wife of Śiva, and is addressed as Umā. There is no longer the same emphasis on her chastity. Arjuna's is primarily a prayer for victory in battle. The hymn of Yudhishṭhira is more general in its application.

> Thou art ever followed by Brahmā and other Devas.
> By those who call upon Thee to lighten their burdens,
> As by those who salute Thee at dawn of day,
> Nothing is unattainable either by way of wealth or children.
> Thou art called Durgā by all because Thou savest men from difficulty.
> Whether in dangerous lands or sinking in the great ocean,
> Thou art the sole refuge of men.
> When assailed by robbers, when crossing streams and seas,
> As also in wilderness and great forests,
> Those who remember Thee, O Mahādevī! are never lost.
> Thou art fame, prosperity, constancy, success and modesty,
> Intelligence, knowledge and man's offspring.[1]

These passages are usually dated in the third or fourth century A.D.,[2] and seem clear evidence that a Durgā sect was already well established. The *Harivaṁśa*, which is a continuation of the epic, dated in the fourth century, also contains references which show the popularity of the goddess, and that she was identified with all the chief deities, and had stolen their characteristic epithets.[3]

It was probably during the succeeding period, that is, about the time of the Gupta Empire, which has been compared with the Periclean age in Greece and the Elisabethan and Stuart eras in England, that the Śākta cult most rapidly spread. It is known to have been a period characterised by reaction from the prevailing Buddhism.[4] The Sāṅkhya philosophy, which is closely linked with certain types of Śākta thought,

[1] Avalon, *Hymns to the Goddess*, pp. 70, 71. For a translation of Arjuna's hymn, and the legend connecting the goddess with Kṛishṇa, see, *ibid.*, p. 114 f. Most of the Sanskrit text and translations are in Muir, *OST*, IV, pp. 433, 425, 432.

[2] Mazumdar: 'Durgā, Her Origin and History,' *JRAS*, 1906, p. 355, suggests a date as late as the seventh or eighth centuries for these passages.

[3] Cp. Chaps. LIX and CLXVI; Muir, *OST*, IV, p. 433 f.; Avalon, *Hymns*, p. 82 f.

[4] V. A. Smith, *EHI*, p. 320.

appeared in an early form centuries before, but the primary authority in regard to it, the *Sāṅkhya-kārikā*, dates from about this time. The legends connected with the goddess received much attention in popular literature. Kālidāsa, for example, prince of Sanskrit poets and dramatists, probably flourished under Chandragupta II of Ujjain, who ruled early in the fifth century A.D., and among his works is the *Kumārasambhava*, a refined and polished epic which relates the story of Umā's marriage with Śiva.

From the sixth century, and possibly earlier, comes the *Devīmāhātmya* or *Chaṇḍīmāhātmya* or *Saptaśati*, which has been interpolated in the *Mārkaṇḍeya Purāṇa* (81–93). It celebrates the mighty deeds of the goddess, and refers to her daily worship and autumn festival. The work is still very popular, and is described by Barth as 'the principal sacred text of the worshippers of Durgā in Northern India.'[1] In it there are many traces of magical beliefs, and descriptions of the terrifying appearance of the goddess, but appeals are also made to her tenderer aspects, and a deep faith in her power is evidenced. It must have originated in some place dedicated to the goddess in one of her terrible forms, but not in Bengal. Pargiter, the editor of the standard critical English edition of the text, connects it with Mandhata in Western India.[1] It tells in graphic language of the vanquishing of the gods by Mahisha and his demons. Out of the special energies of all the deities a goddess is formed, Chaṇḍikā or Ambikā, and after a great battle she destroys the demon-buffalo and his followers. Later the gods are again overcome, this time by the demons Śumbha and Niśumbha. The former sought to marry the goddess, and when she declined an army was sent against her under Chaṇḍa and Muṇḍa. It was destroyed by the goddess Kālī, who in return received from Chaṇḍikā the name Chamuṇḍā. Chaṇḍikā herself at length conquered Niśumbha and Śumbha, whereat the universe was filled with joy. In this fierce framework there are passages breathing deep religious feeling and enthusiastic adoration.

[1] *Religions of India*, p. 197 n. On the date see Winternitz, *Geschichte der indischen Literatur*, I, p. 473.

O goddess, who removest the sufferings of thy suppliants, be gracious!
Be gracious, O mother of the whole world!
Be gracious, O queen of the universe! safeguard the universe!
Thou, O goddess, art queen of all that is moveable and immoveable!

O goddess, be gracious! Protect us wholly from fear of our foes
Perpetually, as thou hast at this very time saved us promptly by the slaughter of the Asuras!
And bring thou quickly to rest the sins of all the worlds
And the great calamities which have sprung from the maturing of the portents!
To us who are prostrate be thou gracious,
O goddess, who takest away afflictions from the universe!
O thou worthy of praise from the dwellers in the three worlds,
Bestow thou boons on the worlds! (91.)[1]

Shortly after this prayer come the instructions from the goddess to her worshippers:

At the offering of the *bali*, and during worship in the ceremonies with fire, and at a great festival, all this story of my exploits must verily be proclaimed and listened to . . . . And at the great annual worship that is performed in autumn time, the man who listens filled with faith to this poem of my majesty, shall assuredly through my favour be delivered from every trouble and be blessed with riches, grain and children. . . . When men listen to this poem of my majesty, enemies pass to destruction, and prosperity accrues and their family rejoices. . . . Through my power lions and other dangerous beasts, robbers and enemies, from a distance indeed, flee from him who calls to mind this story of my exploits. (92).[1]

The *Chaṇḍīmāhātmya* forms the background of Bāṇa's *Chaṇḍīśataka*, an ode to Chaṇḍī in a hundred verses. Bāṇabhaṭṭa was a Brāhman living at the court of the Emperor Harsha early in the seventh century. All the territory of the Ganges and its tributaries was part of the empire, which stretched from the east to the west coast and had Kanauj as its capital. Bāṇa's *Harshacharita* is a very early attempt at an historical romance, for it is woven out of actual events in the life and reign of his patron; there are vivid pictures of Indian society and of the manners and customs of the period. It appears that Harsha's ancestral religion was connected with Śaivism and Tāntrism, but he was later converted to Buddhism, and ruled always with a broad toleration. Incidental

[1] Pargiter, *The Mārkaṇḍeya Purāṇa*. *Bali* = sacrifice.

allusions enable us to reconstruct a picture of the goddess worship of the time. There are references to human sacrifice and to the sale of human flesh. The help of the goddess is often invoked. The king comes at one time upon 'a grove sacred to Chaṇḍikā, which was parched and waterless from the hot season, and ugly with leafless trees, with the figures of the goddess carved on the trees at the entrance, which received the homage of passing travellers' (63). Similar pictures may be found in Bāṇa's story *Kādambarī.* For example, on his way to Ujjain, capital of Mālwā, Chandrāpiḍa, one of the heroes of the tale, 'beheld in the forest a red flag, near which was a shrine to Durgā, guarded by an old Dravidian hermit, who made his abode thereby. Dismounting, he entered and bent reverently before the goddess, and bowing again after a sunwise turn, he wandered about interested in the calm of the place.'[1] Bāṇa's son, who completed this story after his father's death, says: 'I hail for the completion of the difficult toil of this unfinished tale Umā and Śiva, parents of earth, whose single body, formed from the union of two halves, shows neither point of union nor disunion.'[2]

In this period we find in the literature of Vaishṇavism, Buddhism and Jainism, as well as in works connected with Śiva, traces of Śākta ideas. Farquhar, in his *Outline of the Religious Literature of India,* treats the whole period from A.D. 550 to 900 under the general title 'The Śākta Systems.' There was an increase in the use of magic spells, a new type of hypnotic meditation, a growing belief in the occult, and the thought of the time was permeated by conceptions of power personified as a goddess.

Early in the eighth century came the work of Bhavabhūti, the great Sanskrit dramatist. In *Mālatīmādhava,* a picture of contemporary life, which has been called 'a sort of Indian *Romeo and Juliet* with a happy ending,' there are several allusions to the worship of the goddess.[3] Act V is both horrible and exciting; Mādhava, the hero, tries to win the favour of the ghouls of the cemetery by an offering of human

[1] Translation by Ridding, p. 172. [2] *Ibid.*, p. 182.

[3] See H. H. Wilson, *Hindu Theatre,* II; Macdonell, *History of Sanskrit Literature,* p. 363; Keith, *The Sanskrit Drama,* p. 186.

flesh, and comes upon a temple of Chāmuṇḍā just in time to save his love, Mālatī, from being sacrificed to the goddess by Aghoraṇṭa, the priest, and his acolyte, Kapālakuṇḍalā. Rudolf Otto would no doubt regard the passage as a finely 'numinous' one, but it is the numinous at the primitive demonic level. When Mādhava discovers Mālatī in the temple he cries:

> What luckless chance is this that such a maid
> With crimson garb and garland like a victim
> Adorned for sacrifice, should be the captive
> Of impious wretches. . . . (*Hindu Theatre*, II, 60.)

H. H. Wilson notes that the epithets used in the last line 'indicate little respect for the worshippers of Durgā, and their application, so publicly declared, would lead us to infer that the author's sentiments were those of his age.' A later commentator explains that the sacrifice of Mālatī would have violated the prohibition of female victims, found, for example, in the *Rudhirādhyāya*, and is therefore condemned; but it seems likely that there was at the time in many circles strong reaction from the darker practices of the Tāntrics.

Some kind of reformation in the sect seems to have followed the work of Śaṅkarāchārya, though he was not himself a Śākta in the sectarian sense. His dates are given usually as A.D. 788 to 850, but it is possible that the earlier one is to be understood as the year of his spiritual birth, and that he died about 820. He lived in the south of India, and has been called 'the Thomas Aquinas of Hinduism,'[1] for his fame rests chiefly on his philosophical and controversial works. What exactly were his relations with the Śāktas it is difficult to determine. Numerous Śākta précis in prose and verse, some of them of an unpleasant character, are traditionally ascribed to him. According to Monier Williams, it is known that he placed a representation of the *Śrī-chakra* in each of the four monasteries which he founded.[2] Lakshmīdhara, who lived in the thirteenth, or possibly in the twelfth century, wrote a commentary to the *Saundaryalaharī*, a famous ode

[1] Farquhar, *ORLI*, p. 174. For a brief account of his life and teaching see Cave, *Redemption, Hindu and Christian*, Chap. IV.
[2] *Brahmanism and Hinduism*, p. 203.

to the goddess, and unhesitatingly ascribes it to Śaṅkara. 'Serious scholars,' says Farquhar, 'regard the ascription as a mistake,'[1] but it is suggestive of the strength of the sect that it should be able even to claim such a figure. Arthur and Ellen Avalon translate ten songs which they ascribe to him, among them one with the often-quoted refrain: 'A bad son may be born sometimes, but a bad mother never.' A fine German rendering of this last has been made by Otto von Glasenapp, and his son apparently accepts the tradition which ascribes it to Śaṅkara.[2] Winternitz has said: 'Probably many of these hymns are really his own, though it is likely that the majority are wrongly attributed to him.'[3]

The truth seems to be that Śaṅkara was a Smārta Brāhman, worshipping the five gods, Vishṇu, Śiva, Durgā, Sūrya, and Gaṇeśa. Possibly the Devī as Śāradā, the goddess of wisdom, was his *ishṭa-devatā*, his special protectress, receiving in consequence more attention than the others. From his *Bhāshya* on the *Gita* it appears that he practised Śākta Yoga. He proclaimed a lower kind of truth for ordinary men, and a higher for the philosopher, but he seems to have done all he could to help the movement for the purifying of temples, whether these were Śākta or of other Hindu sects. As an orthodox Brāhman, however, his desire would be to see an increase of *Pañchāyatana* temples. At Conjeeveram, for example, he was able to change the chief priests, and to introduce the worship of the five gods.[4] Before the reform the Conjeeveram temple was probably an old Dravidian one, where Left-hand Śākta worship took place. Afterwards it became Smārta. Incidents like this probably lie behind the traditions connecting him with the beginnings of the *Dakshināchāra* school in Śāktism.

Part of the uncertainty is due to the fact that Śaṅkara is a common name. Govinda Das, when he quotes the following hymn as setting forth the true Āgama view, ascribes it to 'one of the Śaṅkarāchāryas': 'O world-mother, hearken unto me, thy most wayward child. I desire not wealth, nor

[1] *ORLI*, p. 266.
[3] *Hymns to the Goddess*, p. 95; *Indische Gedichte*, p. 55.
[2] *Geschichte der indischen Literatur*, III, p. 122.
[4] See *ORLI*, p. 268; *ERE*, VII, p. 646.

wife, not *mukti* even; but what I do desire is to serve Thee, and Thee only, for the sake of uttermost service alone.'[1]

It is from the seventh century onwards, though possibly from considerably earlier, that the first Śākta *Tantras* date.[2] These are the special scriptures of the sect. 'The Tantra,' says Avalon, 'deals with all matters of common belief and interest, from the doctrine of the origin of the world to the laws which govern kings and the societies which they have been divinely appointed to rule, medicine and science generally.'[3] The dating of particular *Tantras* is a matter of very great difficulty. In the next chapter their characteristics will be more fully described. Here we are concerned with the other literature.

The only Prākṛit drama extant, the *Karpūra-mañjarī* (Camphor-cluster), was written by Rājaśekhara, who seems to have been a Śaiva and to have lived about A.D. 900 in the Western Deccan. The description of the Kaula magician Bhairavānanda has already been quoted. The play also contains an account of the *dolajātra* (swing-festival) of Gaurī. Karpūra-mañjarī, the heroine, is put in a swing in front of the image of Pārvatī. In many places there were much more terrible variations of this method of worship. Men used in some parts to swing with iron hooks fastened into their backs, and in more recent times sheep and other animals have been similarly sacrificed.[4] In the *Karpūra-mañjarī*, however, no such things occur.

From the eleventh and succeeding centuries come several Śākta *Upanishads*, the most famous being the *Kaula*, which is specially connected with the most extreme of the Śāktas. In the general literature of the time the invocation of Śiva and his consort became a favourite literary device, and there are many evidences of the continued popularity of the cult. One of the stories from the *Hitopadeśa* (I. 7) deals with the worship of Gaurī with young girls according to Tāntric rites, and probably originated in Bengal about this time. Another

1 *Hinduism*, p. 126.
2 Glasenapp, *Brahma und Buddha*, p. 149, dates the *Tantras* from about A.D. 500.
3 *Principles of Tantra*, Pt. I, Introduction. p. xxix.
4 Cp. Whitehead, *Village Gods of Southern India*.

famous collection of stories, many of which have penetrated to the West, the *Vetālapañcaviṁśatikā*, or twenty-five tales of the Vetāla, has a framework connecting it with Śākta practices. King Vikrama of Ujjain is directed by an ascetic to carry a corpse from a tree to the graveyard where the magical rites take place, without uttering a word. On the way a Vetāla, a special kind of demon which frequents dead bodies, enters the corpse and begins to tell the king a fairy-tale. Unthinkingly the king replies to a question, and at once his burden disappears and is found hanging on the tree again. The king goes back to fetch it, and the same process is repeated till the Vetāla has told twenty-five tales. In the stories themselves there are references to the worship of the goddess. Tāntric influences are also to be found in the *Siṁhāsanadvātriṁśikā*, or 'Thirty-two Stories of the Lion-seat' (i.e. throne).[1]

Śāktism maintained itself throughout the period of Muhammadan ascendancy, which began in the twelfth century. No doubt from time to time, and from district to district, there was waxing and waning of strength. The *Kālikā Purāṇa* or *Tantra* which is connected especially with Bengal, and contains the famous Blood Chapter, already quoted, giving directions for the offering of human and animal sacrifices to Chaṇḍikā, seems to have been written about the fourteenth century.

Chaṇḍīdās, the famous Bengali poet, who flourished from about 1380 to 1420, has sometimes been regarded as a Śākta. His name means 'servant of the goddess,' and he inherited from his father the position of priest of the temple of Vāśulī Devī in his birthplace in the Birbhum district. But he came under Buddhist Tāntric influences, and after being persecuted for a love affair with a washer-woman became a devotee of the cult of Rādhā and Kṛishṇa. 'All his poems,' says Mrs. Margaret Macnicol, 'are Vaishṇava.'[2] The songs of Chaṇḍīdās, which deal with every phase of human love, were the inspiration of the great Vaishṇava reformer, Chaitanya (1485–1533), who reacted strongly from the licentiousness of

[1] On these collections of stories see Winternitz, *Geschichte der indischen Literatur*, III.

[2] *Poems by Indian Women*, p. 72. Cp. D. C. Sen, *HBLL*.

the worship of his time, and who communicated his enthusiasm to Śaṅkara Deva, who started a similar reformation in Assam, attacking the Śākta practices there generally accepted.[1]

Though we cannot reckon Chaṇḍīdās among them, yet the Śāktism of Bengal has produced several poets, who in hymns of great power and charm have celebrated the goddess in all her varying moods. Their work constitutes one of the most interesting phenomena connected with the sect. Among the more famous are Mukundarāma, sometimes known as *Kavikaṅkan* or 'gem of poets,' who finished his chief poem, the epic *Chaṇḍī*, in 1589, Rām Prasād Sen (1718–1775), who has been described as 'a bee intoxicated with the honey of the lotus feet of *Śakti*,'[2] and Bhārata Chandra Ray (1722–1760), a court-poet. Conditions in Bengal, from which these singers drew much of their inspiration, will be considered in greater detail later on.

In the eighteenth century the sect extended its hold over the popular imagination. 'The eighteenth century,' it has been said, 'saw the lines of traditional mediæval Hinduism hardening again with almost unrelieved darkness. The grossest forms of impure worship flourished unrebuked. This was especially the case in Bengal, where the unclean Tāntric rites, connected with Kālī worship, spread with alarming rapidity. The first advent of the British did nothing to check the evil.'[3] Bhāskararāya (or Bhāskarānandanatha), a well-known commentator on some of the earlier *Tantras*, lived in the early decades of the century. He was court pundit in Tanjore, and probably a Śrauta or Smārta Brāhman. Several important new *Tantras* were produced, including the one best known in the West, the *Mahānirvāṇa Tantra*, which, though belonging to the Left-hand school, is fitly described as 'a noble work.'[4]

The early years of the nineteenth century saw the birth of reform movements within Hinduism. These were stimulated

[1] Eliot, *Hinduism and Buddhism*, II, p. 259, suggests that Śaṅkara may have been quite independent of Chaitanya.
[2] *Principles of Tantra*, p. 25.
[3] C. F. Andrews, *The Renaissance in India*, pp. 101–2.
[4] Farquhar, *ORLI*, p. 354.

by the increasing contact between East and West. Many of the more revolting practices disappeared, or were suppressed; a nobler conception of the divine was evident. More recently, however, there has been renewed interest in Śākta principles. Avalon in his books refers to the work of several Śākta theologians, and has translated the *Tantratattva*, or *Principles of Tantra*, written by one of them. The practices of the sect have been described in several of the novels of Bankim Chatterji (1838–94), the first B.A. of Calcutta University.[1] *Kapālakuṇḍalā*, a story of the time of Akbar, and *Ānanda Maṭh*, an eighteenth century tale, are the best known. The latter has achieved very great fame by reason of a hymn to the Mother (*Bande Mātaram*) which it contains, and which has been used as a kind of national anthem by Bengali patriots, first during the disputes regarding the partition of the province and more recently in the agitation for self-government. The influence of Śākta ideas on certain phases of the *swarāj* movement will be described at greater length in a subsequent chapter. In recent times there has been a rehabilitation of many Hindu beliefs which thirty years ago would have been explained away or repudiated. Chief among these are those connected with *Śākti*, and round this revival a new popular literature has sprung up.

[1] For some account of Chatterji's work see Frazer, *A Literary History of India*, pp. 419–29.

CHAPTER V

THE TANTRAS

IT is only during the present century that the *Tantras*, the special literature of the Śāktas, have been seriously studied in the West, and at present the materials available are not large. In 1900 Manmatha Nath Dutt published in Calcutta an English translation of the first part of the *Mahānirvāṇa Tantra*. The same year Dr. John Murdoch, of Madras, persuaded Dr. K. S. Macdonald, a missionary of the Free Church of Scotland, to gather material on the *Tantras* with a view to their critical examination. Before his death, in 1903, Macdonald had secured analyses and translations of a number of *Tantras* from his friends, but, except for a few short articles and pamphlets, had not been able to publish the results of his work. Happily some of the material he collected was preserved, and passed into the possession of Dr. Farquhar. It is known as the *Macdonald MSS.*[1] Since 1913 a series of Tāntric texts have been issued at regular intervals under the general editorship of Arthur Avalon, who in several cases has supplied an English translation or analysis, introduction and notes. There are already some eleven volumes in this series.

A good many misconceptions have arisen owing to the difficulty of access to the *Tantras* themselves. The word *Tantra* has various meanings; starting from that of web or warp,[2] it came gradually to stand for an uninterrupted series, orderly ritual, the doctrinal theory or system itself, and finally its literary exposition. It need not necessarily refer

[1] See J. M. Macphail, *Life of K. S. Macdonald, M.A., D.D.*, pp. 267–71, 291 f. Most of the articles were published in *The Indian Witness*. To the Macdonald MSS., through the courtesy of Dr. Farquhar, I had access, and several of them are now in my possession.

[2] Cp. *SS*, p. 17.

to a religious *Śāstra*. One of the most famous Indian collections of fables, which was certainly known in the fifth century, is called the *Pañchatantra*, since it is divided into five books. Amongst the most influential of the later Sanskrit grammars was the *Kātantra* of Śarvavarman, whose date is uncertain. When the word is applied to a religious work it is not limited to those of the Śāktas. One of the most important methods of Vedic exegesis was the *Karma Mīmāṁsā*, and in the early eighth century the scholar Kumārila produced a work belonged to this school known as the *Tantra-vārttika*, a prose commentary on a work some centuries older by Śabara. To the same literature belongs the *Tantra-ratna*, a commentary produced about 1300. About the same time the sect known as the Mādhvas sprang up in opposition to the Vedantism of Śaṅkara; among the works of the founder, Madhva (1199–1278), is the *Tantrasāra*, a treatise on ritual. Further, in Kashmir Śaivism we find the *Tantrāloka*, produced about 1000, a general work on Śaivism by Abhinava Gupta, who in some of his writings quotes from certain of the Śākta *Tantras*. These examples are sufficient to show that the word was widely used in literary circles.[1]

It is now commonly understood to denote that body of religious scripture which is stated to have been revealed by Śiva as the specific scripture for the fourth Kali age, in which the world now is. According to Hindu chronology, we are living in the last stage of a *Kalpa*, hastening downwards to utter destruction.[2] Each age has its specially revealed scripture. The distinction between *Tantras* and *Purāṇas* is not always well marked. Both are didactic and sectarian. As a rule *Tantras* contain less historical and legendary matter, and more directions as to ritual, but a more important difference lies in this, that while the *Purāṇas* approve of Vedic rites as well as of others, for which they give directions, the *Tantras* insist that ceremonies other than those they prescribe are now useless. In the *Mahānirvāṇa Tantra* (II, 15) Śiva declares: 'The fool who would follow other doctrines heedless of mine is as great a sinner as a parricide

[1] For further information about the works mentioned, see Farquhar, *ORLI*; and Macdonell, *Sanskrit Literature*.

[2] Cp. Underhill, *Hindu Chronology*.

or the murderer of a Brāhman or of a woman. . . . The Vedic rites and *mantras* which were efficacious in the first age have ceased to have power in this. They are now as powerless as snakes whose fangs have been drawn and are like dead things.'[1] Certainly in practice the *Tantras* have superseded the *Vedas* in authority over a large part of India.

There are Buddhist *Tantras* as well as Hindu *Tantras*, Vaishṇava *Tantras* as well as Śākta ones. The common element seems to be that they are all the expression of a system of magical and sacramental ritual which professes to attain the highest aims of religion by means of spells, diagrams, gestures and other physical methods. Tāntrism represents, in the words of Eliot, 'a simplification of religion, but on mechanical rather than emotional lines.'[2] Gilmore expresses somewhat the same idea when he refers to it as a revolt which has as its avowed object 'the reduction of the effort required to reach what in the Hindu system is equivalent to our 'salvation' by suiting that effort to present human ability.'[3]

Eliot, in his work *Hinduism and Buddhism*, makes a distinction between Tāntrism and Śāktism which is in some respects a useful one,[4] but it should be noted that the continued influence of the Tāntric system depends almost entirely on its association with the worship of a goddess or goddesses, and that historically it is not easy to separate the two movements. Even Tāntric Buddhism is permeated with Śākta ideas, and in Hinduism it is only the Śākta *Tantras* that have proved of great influence.

There is no authoritative canon of this literature. In certain *Tantras*, written apparently before the tenth century, lists of sixty-four are given. In the *Āgama-tattva-vilāsa*, a late eighteenth century work, there is a further list of eighty-three. Avalon quotes from the *Mahāsiddhasāra Tantra* a list in three sections, corresponding to a threefold division of India and adjoining lands, and this catalogue also would appear to date

1 *TGL*, pp. 16–17. Cp. *Kulārṇava T.*, I, p. 79 f.; *Tantrasāra* (*Macdonald MSS.*), p. 3.

2 *Hinduism and Buddhism*, II, p. 275. Cp. Glasenapp, *Brahma und Buddha*, p. 156.

3 'Tantrism—the New Hinduism,' *AJT*, XXIII, p. 440.

4 op. cit., I, xxxvi; II, Chap. XXXII, etc.

from the late eighteenth century. The first group contains the *Tantras* of the region *Vishṇukrāntā* (from the Vindhya mountains to Chittagong, that is, in particular, Bengal). Then come those of the region *Rāthakrāntā* (from the Vindhya mountains to China, that is, apparently, Northern India), and thirdly those of the region *Aśvakrāntā* (the rest of India).[1] Among the *Macdonald MSS.* is a note by Satis Chandra Vidyābhūshaṇa, which, after giving a list of sixty-four titles from the *Mahāviśvasāra Tantra*, continues: 'Besides these there are a hundred other *Tantras.* There is mention of another batch of sixty-two in the *Vārāhī Tantra.* The Buddhists mention seventy-two of their own.' An interesting list, of value because of its date and source, is to be found in *The History, Literature, and Mythology of the Hindoos*, issued in 1810 by William Ward, the Serampore missionary.[2] These different catalogues vary so greatly, and so many of the works to which they refer appear to be lost, that at present they are not of much help to the student. Only a very few can be dated with any certainty, and no satisfactory classification has yet been suggested. 'The whole literature,' as Farquhar has said, 'awaits the toil of scholarly investigators.'[3] There are, in addition to the *Tantras*, other closely allied Śākta treatises and compendia.

In spite of this confusion, however, certain *Tantras* are well attested and have obviously had great influence. The general characteristics of the literature can be determined. The word *Tantra* is not used in its specialised sense of a religious treatise in the *Amarakośa*, the great Sanskrit dictionary, which was probably composed about A.D. 500.[4] Avalon, in sympathy, apparently, with those Śāktas who insist on the great antiquity of their texts, argues that the silence of the *Amarakośa* proves little, as there are other omissions from it.[5] A more important piece of evidence is found, however, in the fact that the Chinese pilgrims, who visited India between A.D. 400 and 700, and have left revealing accounts of the political and religious conditions during those centuries,

[1] *TT*, I, ii; iv, 4. Cp. *Principles of Tantra*, I, pp. lxv–lxvii.
[2] op. cit., II, p. 362 f. [3] *ORLI*, p. 199.
[4] Macdonell, *Sanskrit Literature*, p. 433.
[5] *Principles of Tantra*, Introduction, p. xxi.

make no reference to Tāntric literature.[1] It seems safe to assume, therefore, that the *Tantras* did not take definite shape before the seventh century, though many of the *mantras* and hymns which they include may be of very much earlier date. From the seventh until the eighteenth century there was a steady stream of these works, and of commentaries upon them.

The *Tantras* are regarded traditionally as the revelation of the three supreme deities, Brahmā, Vishṇu and Śiva, but in form they are dependent upon Śiva alone, and almost invariably consist of a dialogue in which Śiva, in answer to the questions of his wife, upholds the mysteries of the sect. Avalon distinguishes between *Āgama* and *Nigama* forms of *Tantras*; in the former Śiva acts as *guru*, while in the latter the Devī instructs in reply to the questions of her lord. The range of subjects treated is encyclopædic. The *Tantras* are the storehouse of Indian occultism, they are the chief authorities on *yoga* practice, they deal with all branches of worship, there is in them a considerable amount of philosophical material. Avalon sums up their contents in the following catalogue: 'The Supreme Spirit, the creation and destruction of the universe, the origin and worship of the *devas*, classification of beings, the heavenly bodies, descriptions of the worlds and hells, of man and woman, and of the centres (*chakra*) of the human body, the law and duty (*dharma*) of the different ages, and of the stages of life in the individual called *āśrama*, the sacraments, the consecration of images of *devatā*, *mantra*, *yantra*, *mudrā*, all forms of spiritual training (*sādhanā*) and worship (*pūjā*, *upāsana*), whether external or mental, including worship with the *pañchatattva*, consecration of houses, lands, wells, trees, etc., descriptions of holy shrines (*tirtha*), *puraścharana*, *japa*, *vrata*, *shatkarma-sādhanā*, and all forms of ceremonial rites and "magic," meditation (*dhyāna*) and *yoga*, the duties of kings, law, custom, magic and science generally.'[2] This characteristically

[1] Cp. Eliot, *Hinduism and Buddhism*, II, 125.

[2] *Principles of Tantra*, Introduction, p. lxii f. *Puraścharana* = a rite for the invigoration of *mantras*; very full instructions are to be found in the *Tantrasāra*. *Japa* = repetition of *mantras*. *Vrata* = festivals, such as the Durgā *pūjā*. *Shatkarmasādhanā* = purification.

confused list shows how varied are the subjects treated in the *Tantras*. Whether there is in them anything of great scientific or historical value is at present not very certain. If there is, it seems likely to be in the realm of physiology. V. G. Rele has recently said: 'The anatomy of nerves in the Tāntric manuals compares favourably with our present knowledge of them.'[1]

An interesting parallel to the many-sidedness of the Tāntric speculations is furnished by some of the Jewish apocalyptic writings. The contents is similarly heterogeneous in character. World history is symbolically represented in the Enoch literature, for example, together with ethical and religious teaching, crude astronomy, theories about sun, moon, stars, winds, etc., folklore regarding demons, magic, and crude physiological and medical speculations. Most of it consorts strangely with Jewish monotheism, and was probably learned from Babylonia. Such apocalyptic tracts were the Tantras of Judaism, and, without forcing the parallel, when the historical background in Bengal is considered in greater detail, we shall see reasons for the suggestion that Śāktism fed upon the same kind of uncertainty and despair as did the apocalyptic movement.

Among the best-known and most quoted of *Tantras* are the *Rudra-yāmala*, which appears to date from the tenth or eleventh century, and is used by H. H. Wilson in his account of *Vāmāchāra* worship; the *Kulārṇava T.*, which is referred to by Lakshmīdhara, a scholar who lived towards the end of the thirteenth century;[2] the *Prapañchasāra T.*, sometimes wrongly attributed to Śaṅkara, but dated by Farquhar some centuries later and described as 'rather a foul book,' though it contains, as J. W. Hauer notes, a profound philosophy of language;[3] the *Śāradātilaka T.*, a work of very great authority, written by Lakshmaṇa Deśika, a scholar belonging to the

[1] *The Mysterious Kundalini*, p. 33. Cp. Max Weber, *Gesammelte Aufsätze zur Religionssozilogie*, II, p. 166: 'In übrigen hat die Tantra-Literatur hier alchemistische, auf dem Gebiet der Medizin aber vor allem anatomische, speziell nervenanatomische Kenntnisse von ganz erheblichem Umfang gezeigt.'

[2] *TT*, V, Introduction by Avalon.

[3] *ORLI*, p. 266; *TT*, III. Cp. Hauer, *Die Dhāraṇī im nördlichen Buddhismus*, p. 8 n.

eleventh century, and dealing almost entirely with spells and sorcery;[1] the *Kaula Upanishad*, already referred to as one of the chief scriptures of the extremer Śāktas;[2] the *Yoginī T.*, which appears to mention the Koch king Vishṇusiṁha, who reigned from about 1515 to 1540, and is clearly connected with Kāmarūpa;[3] and the *Mahānirvāṇa T.*, produced in Bengal probably in the last half of the eighteenth century, and admitted by all to be a really great work, though it belongs the Left- rather than the Right-hand school.

The *Mahānirvāṇa* or 'Tantra of the Great Liberation,' is the *Tantra* best known in the West, and deservedly. The first two chapters are introductory. Mount Kailasa is described; there Pārvatī finds her husband, and, after recounting the story of the three past ages of the world cycle, ascribes to him the revelations of the Vedic scriptures, reminds him of the characteristics of the present era, and beseeches him to give directions 'how, without great pains, men may obtain longevity, health, energy, strength and courage, learning, intelligence and happiness; how they may become great in strength and valour, pure of heart, obedient to parents . . . mindful of the good of their neighbour, reverent to the *devas*.'[4] Śiva replies that salvation is no longer obtainable through *Vedas* and *Purāṇas*, but by the *Tantras* alone, which contain, in addition to newer ritual, the essence of all preceding revelation. A noble passage on the worship of the one supreme, eternal and omnipresent God follows. In chapter III the exposition of worship and its method begins, and at once reference is made to *mantras*, and the conditions necessary for their effective repetition. Śiva declares Devī mother of the universe in the next chapter, and her worship as Creatrix, Protectress and Destroyer as necessary for salvation in the Kali age. How *mantras* may be formed, and the ritual of the placing of the jar, is described in chapter V, and in the following one there are directions for *pañchatattva* worship. Next comes a hymn to Kālī, containing a hundred of her names all beginning with K.[5] Chapter VIII is

[1] Introduction and analysis by Ewing, *JAOS*, XXIII (1902).
[2] Cp. 'Saktaic Literature,' *SJM*, III (1897).
[3] Translation by Munro in the *Macdonald MSS.*
[4] *TGL*, p. 4. [5] Cp. *Hymns to the Goddess*, p. 54.

important for its attractive picture of the life of the householder, its regulations for the forming of circles for worship, and its account of the duties of the ascetic. There are many things in the chapter which recall the Code of Manu, passages from the *Bhagavadgītā* and some of the Buddhist sermons.[1] The rites of purification and consecration in connection with the various stages of life are given in chapters IX and X. Except for some of the marriage instructions in connection with *chakra* worship, there are few divergences from accepted Hindu practice in these matters. Chapter XI defines various crimes and their punishments, while chapter XII has to do with relationships, inheritance, gifts, property and trading. A fine conception of the sacredness of life in all its phases, and a keen desire for ethical conduct is evident amid detailed instructions which are often difficult to understand. Chapter XIV begins with regulations for the erection of the *liṅgam*, the symbol of Śiva, and ends with a eulogy of all that has gone before.

Such an analysis, brief though it is, indicates the general contents and method of the best of the *Tantras*. The *Mahānirvāṇa T.* was probably written at the end of the eighteenth century. The earliest extant commentary is by Hariharānanda Bhāratī, one of the pundits of Rām Mohan Ray, who died in 1833. In view of its condemnation of widow-burning, Gilmore thinks it was written, or perhaps revised, about the middle of the nineteenth century.[2] But attempts had been made to suppress *sati* from within Hinduism many years before the British took action, and the references in the *Mahānirvāṇa Tantra* in no way involve a nineteenth century date. All the other evidence also is against Gilmore's contention.

The *Tantrasāra*, or Essence of Tantra, is a work somewhat similar in spirit to the *Mahānirvāṇa T.*, and was produced in Bengal about the same time. Among the *Macdonald MSS.* is a partial translation by McCulloch and Chatterji. It is to be described as a Tāntric compendium rather than as a *Tantra*. According to Farquhar, the author was one Kṛishṇā-

[1] Cp. Winternitz, *Ostasiatische Zeitschrift,* IV, p. 158.
[2] *AJT,* XXIII (1919), p. 457. Cp. Edward Thompson, *Suttee.*

nanda Vāgīśa, and it was compiled in 1812.[1] Avalon quotes an Indian scholar who connects the *Tantrasāra* with a Kṛishṇānanda Bhaṭṭāchārya, whom he regards as a contemporary of Chaitanya.[2] The subject is further complicated by references in Ronaldshay's *Heart of Aryavarta* to Kṛishṇānanda Āgamvāgīśa, 'the first expounder of Tantras in Bengal,' a pupil of Vasudeva Sarvabhauma, who in the fifteenth century established a school of Logic at Navadvipa.[3] Without accepting a sixteenth century date for the work, we can confidently maintain that 1812, as suggested by Farquhar, is too late, for it is quoted by William Ward in *The History, Literature and Mythology of the Hindoos*, the first edition of which appeared towards the close of 1810.[4]

The *Tantrasāra* contains several fine hymns, some of them quoted from older Tāntric works. In certain passages magical ideas are prominent, and virtue is said to be acquirable by the mere repetition of the hymns; in others the chief aim seems to be to make the worshipper meditate on the physical form of the goddess; but at times a much higher level is reached, as, for example, in the stanza:

> O Bhawānī! the *munis* describe thee in physical form
> The *śruti* speaks of thee in subtle form;
> Others again call thee the presiding deity of speech;
> Others again as the root of the worlds;
> But we think of thee
> As the untraversable ocean of mercy, and nothing else.[5]

At the beginning of the work someone who calls himself merely Kṛishṇānanda states his intention of giving the essence of Tāntric teaching. He describes the characteristics necessary in a *guru*, and the way he should be reverenced. 'If Śiva is angered, the preceptor is a deliverer; if the preceptor is angered, there is no deliverer.'[6] The disciple must not be illiterate, miserly, sinful or irreligious, but once he has

[1] *ORLI*, pp. 355, 389.
[2] *Principles of Tantra*, Introduction, p. xliv.
[3] op. cit., p. 36. He seems to be following a monograph on *Logic in the University of Nadia*, by S. C. Vidyabhusana.
[4] e.g. II, 365, 267; III, 93.
[5] *Hymns to the Goddess*, p. 20. Several other hymns are there quoted.
[6] McCulloch, *Macdonald MSS.*, p. 1.

entrusted himself to a *guru*, on the latter rests the responsibility for any sins he may commit. Only Tāntric rites, it is emphasised, are efficacious in the Kali *yuga*. There follow complicated rules for the use of *mantras*. Days and places favourable for initiation are described; rosaries and how they should be consecrated; *pūjā* with *mantras*, *yantras*, and *mudrās*. A number of *yantras*, *chakras*, and *maṇḍalas*[1] are reproduced and explained. Among other works the following are quoted: the *Rudrayāmala T.*, the *Kulachūḍāmaṇi T.*, and the *Kulārṇava T.*, all of which seem to belong to the tenth or eleventh centuries, the *Yoginī T.*, and the *Vārāhī T.*, which are probably sixteenth century works, and the *Kriyāsāra*, which may be the manual of that name by Nīlakaṇṭha, which is dated about 1650.[2] There is also a reference to Nityānanda, perhaps the disciple of Chaitanya who introduced an easier discipline into the Vaishṇava orders and so contributed to their flooding by converts from the degraded Śākta Buddhists.

The *Śāktānanda-taraṅginī*, an important treatise on the ritual, which Farquhar dates after 1821, must also be placed some years earlier, as it occurs in William Ward's list of 'Treatises on Religious Ceremonies.'[3]

Among the *Macdonald MSS.* there are translations of the *Kāmadhenu Tantra* and the *Mantrakośa*, both of them eighteenth century works dealing with the correct use of *mantras*. The introduction to the *Tantrakalpadruma* is also given; this appears to be a Bengali compilation which aims at popularising knowledge of the *Tantras* by translating them from the Sanskrit into the vernacular. The *Mahānirvāṇa Tantra* is quoted, and a list of other works. The introduction is dated 1305 Bengali era, that is, A.D. 1898.

Enough has been said to indicate the general character of Tāntric works. The *Tantras* claim to be a scripture for all and lay little stress on caste. They insist that the text and ritual can be properly understood only after initiation and with the help of a *guru*. The ritual, which aims

[1] Cp. Zimmer, *Kunstform und Yoga*, p. 26 f., and Plates.
[2] *ORLI*, pp. 350, 353, 385. Cp. *TT*, IV and V.
[3] Ward, op. cit., II, p. 364; *ORLI*, p. 389. Analysis by Herbert Anderson among the *Macdonald MSS.*

less at beseeching than compelling the goddess, consists chiefly in the correct use of spells, magical or sacramental syllables and letters, diagrams and gestures. The worshipper seeks union with the divine, seeks indeed to become divine. It is believed that man is a microcosm corresponding to the macrocosm of the universe. Many of the ideas found in the *Tantras* are widespread among other Hindu sects, and are not distinctively Śākta. Apart from the ceremonial taught, many of the general principles laid down breathe a liberal and intelligent spirit. That caste distinctions are so minimised may, as Glasenapp has suggested, point to the strong influence of non-Aryan ideas.[1] Women are honoured, and can act as teachers. The burning of widows is forbidden, and girl widows are allowed to re-marry.[2] The murder of a woman is regarded as a particularly heinous crime. Prostitution is denounced. There is considerable truth in the remark which Eliot makes in *Hinduism and Buddhism*: 'Whereas Christianity is sometimes accused of restricting its higher code to church and Sundays, the opposite may be said of Tāntrism. Outside the temple its morality is excellent.'[3]

In spite, however, of these favourable features, the *Tantras* cannot be regarded as great literature. Their philosophical and theological parts lack originality. The magic and erotic parts have no distinction of style. Eliot's considered judgment is worth quoting: 'However much new Tāntric literature may be made accessible in future, I doubt if impartial criticism will come to any opinion except that Śāktism and Tāntrism collect and emphasize what is superficial, trivial and even bad in Indian religion, omitting and neglecting its higher sides. If, for instance, the *Mahānirvāṇa Tantra*, which is a good specimen of these works, be compared with Śaṅkara's commentary on the *Vedānta sūtras*, or the poems of Tulsīdās, it will be seen that it is woefully deficient in the excellencies of either. But many Tāntric treatises are chiefly concerned with charms, spells, amulets, and other magical methods of obtaining wealth, causing or averting disease and destroying enemies, processes which, even if effi-

[1] *Brahma und Buddha*, p. 151.
[2] Cp. e.g. *Mahānirvāṇa T.*, X, 79; XI, 67. *TGL*, pp. 245, 269.
[3] op. cit., II, p. 285.

cacious, have nothing to do with the better side of religion.'[1] The *Tantras* not merely sanction the lowest rites of primitive savagery and superstition, they are guilty of the crime of seeking philosophical justification for such things.

[1] op. cit., II, p. 283. The *Rāmacharit-mānasa* of Tulsīdās (1532–1623) popularised *bhakti* in North India. His poems should be compared with those of Rām Prasād rather than with the *Tantras*. Jewish Apocalyptic literature or *Leviticus* appears 'woefully deficient' beside the *Psalms*. After some more than usually appreciative remarks on the *Tantras*, Winternitz, *Ostasiatische Zeitschrift*, IV, p. 160, says: 'Zum grösseren Teil enthalten diese Werke doch nur Stumpfsinn und Kauderwelsch.'

CHAPTER VI

NON-ARYAN INFLUENCES FAVOURING ŚĀKTISM

SOME of the possible causes of the growth of Śāktism and and Tāntrism must now be considered. Many of the ideas and practices cannot be traced back directly to the *Ṛigveda*, but they permeated mediæval Hinduism, and have had great influence in modern times. Some explanation of this must be sought. An older generation was inclined to dismiss the phenomena in horror and disgust, with no attempt to understand their origin. Where reasons were suggested they can hardly now be regarded seriously. For example, J. N. Bhaṭṭāchārya, writing late in the last century, said: 'To me it seems that the Tāntric cult was invented partly to justify the habit of drinking, which prevailed among the Brāhmans even after the prohibition of it by our great lawgivers, but chiefly to enable the Brahmanical courtiers of the beastly kings to compete with the secular courtiers in the struggle of becoming favourites, and causing the ruin of their royal masters.'[1] Avalon tells us that 'whilst every form of knowledge has its use, the Indian mind rightly apprizes as of the highest value the world of ideas, deeming the question of their "historical" origins and development to be, as in fact it is, of much inferior importance.'[2] His own adoption of this attitude is one of the chief weaknesses of his work, for only in the light of its history can the real significance and meaning of a belief be understood.

India seems to be unique in showing a higher appreciation of goddesses in its later religious development than

[1] *Hindu Castes and Sects*, p. 413.
[2] *Principles of Tantra*, Pt. II, Preface, p. vii.

in its earlier. In most cases, also, the worship of the reproductive forces of Nature is a matter of ancient history. Today in China and Japan, as formerly in Greece and Rome, it has decayed as civilisation advanced, and has ceased to be an important constituent of religion. It is only in India, and to some extent in Tibet, which has been influenced by India, that such worship has continued unashamed until modern times. Starbuck has pointed out that in other parts of the world the worship of goddesses was combined with agricultural pursuits, usually in protected valleys; through the fusion of clans and cities into warring nations 'in which chivalry and virility are at a premium, male deities have risen supreme, while those of the "weaker sex" have been degraded to lesser functions, attached as consorts, superseded and forgotten, or, to save themselves, have changed their sex to fit the new demands.'[1] He suggests that, in spite of the apparent contradiction in the case of India, the same principle is there illustrated, but in a negative way. 'The *Vedas* were written before and during the period when the Aryans were conquering the aborigines of India and were engaged in feuds among their own tribes. Under such conditions there are no goddesses, although the literature is richly polytheistic. Since the nation has settled down into a relatively peaceful life and agricultural pursuits, the worship of female deities has risen to a place of supreme importance; Durgā, the spirit of Nature and Spring; Kālī, soul of infinity and eternity; Sarasvatī, supreme wisdom; and Śākti, mother of all phenomena.'[2] Starbuck notes further, as contributing to this change, the high position accorded to women from the earliest times. The problem is not, however, as simple as Starbuck suggests, nor are his remarks accurate. There are Vedic goddesses, though, as we have seen, they are not of great importance. Certainly the parts where goddess worship has been most prevalent have not been those where life has been 'relatively peaceful.' Some of the more extraneous causes which may have been at work must be considered.

[1] 'Female Principle,' *ERE*, V, 828.

[2] *Ibid.* The derivation of Kālī from *Kala* (time) is very uncertain; it is more likely a late connection.

Śāktism is most commonly regarded as the product of the influence of non-Aryan elements on Aryan religion. There are, however, several different and conflicting variations of this theory. Moreover, it is becoming increasingly clear that Winternitz is right in emphasising the fact that animal and demon cults and fetishism must not be unquestioningly labelled 'non-Aryan,' as has often been done in the past.[1] Aryan religion had its lower and darker side, and not all the unpleasant practices and beliefs of Hinduism came from the conquered peoples. J. W. Hauer, in his interesting and important researches into the problem of the *Vrātya* and the non-Brahmanical side of Aryan religion, has shown how close are the parallels between some of the old sacrifices, like that of the *Mahāvrata* and many of the ceremonies which repel us in the *Tantras*.[2] But that non-Aryan influences played a very large part in the development of Śāktism is clear.

It is sometimes urged that the worship of female deities was introduced, or at any rate popularised, by peoples who entered India from Asia after the main Aryan immigration. We are told by D. A. Mackenzie, for example, that a revolution in the Hindu pantheon took place during the Brahmanic age as a result of the rise of the 'Middle Kingdom,' which was inhabited by a group known as the Bhāratas, who worshipped Bhāratī, a goddess not unlike the mother-goddesses of Egypt and early Europe; that this goddess became associated with Sarasvatī, and was ultimately recognised as the wife of Brahmā, the supreme god; that when Buddhism declined and Śiva became the most popular deity, this goddess-worship was transferred to his consort and was organised into a separate sect.[3] Others have tried to connect the great change which came over Hinduism with the migrations of the nomad nations of the Central Asian steppes, which culminated in the Kushan or Indo-Scythian conquests in Northern India, and prepared the way for the empire of Kanishka in the second century A.D.[4] Our knowledge of the

[1] *Ostasiatische Zeitschrift*, IV, p. 158.

[2] See *Der Vratya*.

[3] *Indian Myth and Legend*, p. xxxix.

[4] So, e.g. C. F. Andrews, *The Renaissance in India*, p. 78. Or he may there have in mind the suggested Iranian invasions of the third century A.D. But on these see V. A. Smith, *OHI*, p. 9. 'Nothing

movements and characteristics of the different peoples, both in the Brahmanic age and subsequently, is, however, much too slight and confused to allow us to speculate in this manner. Many investigators believe that the linguistic and ethnographic evidence suggests that there were several different Aryan invasions of India, but about religious differences among the independent and warring Aryan states in the plains of the Punjab and the upper basin of the Ganges we know nothing. With regard to the Scythians, even if their transitory power in Northern India considerably influenced the religion of the people—an at present quite unproveable hypothesis—there does not seem any evidence to connect them with Tāntric beliefs and practices. Both these suggestions are too artificial, and fail to explain the hold which Śāktism has had on the more primitive peoples in different parts of India.

A much more plausible theory is that which suggests that Aryan religion was gradually permeated by 'Dravidian' elements, and that to the latter this goddess-worship is to be traced. Gilbert Slater in his book, *The Dravidian Element in Indian Culture*, argues enthusiastically that Indian culture is essentially Dravidian and not Aryan, as is commonly supposed. He regards the people whom the Aryans found in possession of India as a branch of the great Mediterranean race,[1] and as the superiors of their conquerors in all but fighting ability. 'While the Dravidians were Aryanised in language, the Aryans were Dravidianised in culture.'[2] In the south, of course, even the original languages maintained themselves. Slater suggests that Dravidian thought had passed from snake-worship[3] and fear of deities like Muniswami, a malignant

definite has been ascertained about them, if they really occurred.' Eliot, *Hinduism and Buddhism*, II, p. 276, refers to the goddess Anahit, who was worshipped with immoral rites in Bactria and is figured on the coins of the Kushans.

[1] Cp. Glasenapp, *Brahma und Buddha*, p. 39.

[2] op. cit., p. 63.

[3] Cp. C. F. Oldham, 'Serpent Worship in India,' *JRAS*, XXIII. He notes the tendency for sacred Nāginis (female hooded-serpents) to be identified with Durgā. In Bengal, Manasā, the snake-goddess, is a form of Devī. The animal which lives in holes and moves in the darkness has everywhere been identified with chthonic spirits.

spirit with a Puck-like streak of humour, to the conception of a deity 'at once lavish and terrible, fickle and incomprehensible, and therefore female, from whom comes smallpox, cholera and famine, but also rich harvests.'[1] This is the village goddess, who bears innumerable names, and is worshipped with very varied rites all over Southern India. Sometimes her festivals are frequent, sometimes once a year, or even once every twelve years. In places it is only when she seems angry, and there has been failure of the rains or pestilence, that she is propitiated. She rejoices in blood and demands the wholesale sacrifice of male animals, and in particular of the male buffalo. Bishop Whitehead has collected much information about the various local beliefs and ceremonies in his *Village Gods of Southern India.* According to Slater, the characteristics of the village goddess are so similar that 'we can hardly refrain from identifying her with Kālī. Kālī with the rounded limbs, wide hips, swelling breasts, exaggerated waist, and with many arms brandishing weapons, tirelessly dancing, a fit emblem indeed for Nature as she is in India, so bountiful in her kindly moods, so deadly when the whim takes her.'[1]

Dravidian art, it is suggested, may have had direct or indirect contact with the art of Knossos. The unnaturally exaggerated waists of the images in both cults are curiously similar. D. C. Sen has noted that the descriptions of Chaṇḍī and her lions fit one of the Cretan goddesses whose representations have been found.[2] Lions were, of course, common in both India and Europe in early times, and parallels like this need imply no direct connection. Recent excavations, however, such as those in Mohenjo-Daro and Harappa, suggest the possibility of connections between the Dravidians and the Sumerians, and the different civilisations of those distant centuries may have had far more in common than has often been realised.[3]

The primitive cults of the village goddesses are connected, in Slater's opinion, with a period before the discovery of the

[1] Slater, op. cit., pp. 91–92. [2] *HBLL*, p. 297.

[3] Cp. Glasenapp, *Brahma und Buddha*, p. 41 f.; W. Foy, *Uber das indische Yoni-Symbol*, argues that there was contact between India and Egypt about 1500 B.C. The *yoni*-shaped altar is found in both lands.

biological facts relating to paternity. Birth was held to be due to the entry of a spirit into the body of the woman, and from this developed the belief in the transmigration of souls, later supplemented by the doctrine of *karma*. 'The discovery of the biological fact of human paternity created the new gods Śiva and Vishṇu.'[1] Originally, Slater thinks, they were local variants of the same deity, who was primarily a god of procreation. This is all highly speculative. There is, however, according to J. F. Hewitt, evidence in Bengal of a time when marriage was unknown, when the mothers were the responsible parents, and did not live with the fathers of their offspring nor consult them as to education or maintenance. The evidence, he thinks, is strongly corroborated by the widespread hold which *Śākti* worship has secured. Matriarchal tribes were probably conquered by northern immigrants, who made the father their head and leader and established the worship of Śiva, the *liṅga* or father god.[2]

Śiva is connected with the bull, as Kālī is with the buffalo. Slater suggests that possibly, though the Dravidians kept buffaloes and associated them with their goddess of fertility, 'they did not, in the proper sense of the word, breed them, and never learnt from them the biology of the birth of calves; but this knowledge came to them first by observation of the more valued bull and cow,' which the Aryans introduced.[3] It has indeed been urged that the association of Śiva with the bull, and the doctrine of the sacredness of the cow, may have been established in India as a result of contact with Egypt in pre-Aryan times, since phallic worship is mentioned with disapproval in the *Ṛigveda*, and the original form of the mother-goddess in Egypt was the divine cow. Most scholars regard the *liṅga* cult as Dravidian. It is certain that in historical times the Dravidians were addicted to this kind of fetishism, and probably the phallic worshippers, condemned by the singers of the *Ṛigveda* (vii. 21. 5; x. 99. 3), were aborigines. There is considerable divergence of opinion as to the age of the buffalo sacrifices. Bishop Whitehead thinks they go back

[1] Slater, op. cit., p. 103.
[2] *JRAS*, XXV (1893), p. 237 f.
[3] Slater, op. cit., p. 108.

very early indeed, and were characteristic of Dravidian religion,[1] but Elmore, in his *Dravidian Gods in Modern Hinduism*, puts forward the view that they originated at a comparatively late date, long after the Aryan invasion of Northern India, and subsequent to the advance of the conquerers into the south, and their triumph there.

These issues are complicated, difficult of decision, and not of very great importance for our purposes here. Whatever be the origin of a god of procreation, he is naturally associated with a goddess of fertility. Vishṇu became linked with Lakshmī, Śiva with Pārvatī, but from very early times Śiva was also mated with Kālī, Durgā and other wild deities. Slater's account of the development of Indian culture is not always convincing, but he is clearly right in drawing attention to the close connection between the village goddesses of the south and those worshipped by the Śāktas and regarded as forms of the wife of Śiva. Hindu ecleticism has no difficulty in assimilating local cults, and regarding the deities worshipped as manifestations of the chief gods and goddesses of the pantheon. The popularity of Śāktism in many places depends on the hold over the inhabitants of some local worship which has been recognised by Hinduism. Many of the cults point back to a totemistic stage of religion. The village deities are almost all worshipped with animal sacrifices. There are grounds for the suggestion that the name Umā may be connected with *amma*, the common name for the mother-goddesses of the Dravidians.[2] Vincent Smith notes that one of the oldest and most powerful demonesses of the southern races, Kottavai, the victorious one, is now identified with Durgā,[3] and Whitehead tells us that among the Kanarese certain outcaste groups become almost a priestly caste in connection with the worship of the goddess.[4] In the latter case the girls do not marry, but are made *basavīs* (fem. of *basava* = bull), that is, are consecrated to the goddess, and become prostitutes. Many of the names by which Devī is known are not Sanskrit words at all. The name *Vindhya-vāsini*, inhabitant of Vindhya, links her with those mountains

[1] *Village Gods of Southern India.*
[2] Cp. Keith, *Religion of the Veda*, p. 199 f.
[3] *EHI*, p. 457. [4] *Village Gods of Southern India*, p. 44.

where human sacrifice continued well into the nineteenth century as part of the cultus of tribes like the Dravidian Gonds, the Kols and the Uraons.[1] In the *Harivaṁśa* the worship of Durgā is especially connected with savage tribes called Śavaras, Varvaras and Pulindas.[2] B. C. Mazumdar, in *The Aborigines of the Highlands of Central India*, gives the evidence for thinking that ethnically Kols and Śavaras are to be identified, and Pargiter and others have shown that the Pulindas were the people of West and North-West India. Even in Sanskrit literature there is abundant testimony to the non-Aryan connections of the goddess. The passage from Bāṇa's story *Kādambarī*, describing a shrine to Durgā guarded by an old Dravidian hermit, has already been quoted.[3] Govinda Das quotes a standard fifteenth century work, which says that Durgā of Mirzapur is the goddess of the Kiratas and other aboriginal tribes, and is worshipped by Mlechchas, Thugs and others of their dread and infamous kind.[4] The allusions in Prākṛit literature are similar. In the *Gaudavaho*, a Prākṛit poem by Vākpati from the seventh or eighth century,[5] there is a description of a king on a journey from Kanauj on the Ganges to Gauda; he is guided by a Śavar, wearing only a turmeric leaf, to a temple of the dread goddess, where human sacrifice has recently taken place. B. C. Mazumdar suggests that Durgā herself may have been originally a tribal goddess connected with the Vindhya mountains, and worshipped with offerings of wine and blood; perhaps Vindhyavāsini in the process of evolution at the fusion of tribes may have become Durgā, and later have been identified with Pārvatī, wife of Śiva.[6] In many of her representations the goddess is to be seen with a garland of freshly severed heads hanging low round her neck; the heads appear to be those of white men, and it may be that in this form she was a deified princess of the dark-skinned

[1] Perhaps Kols, Uraons and Pulindas were pre-Dravidians.
[2] See Muir, *OST*, IV, 434; Avalon, *Hymns to the Goddess*, p. 83.
[3] See above, p. 42. [4] *Hinduism*, p. 191.
[5] The dates given vary from 650 to 750. See Das, op. cit.; Glasenapp, *Brahma und Buddha*, p. 157; Winternitz, *Geschichte der indischen Literatur*, III, 84.
[6] 'Durgā, Her Origin and History,' *JRAS*, 1906, p. 355.

inhabitants of the Vindhya hills, who fought against the fairer incoming Aryans. The name Kālī, as has already been pointed out, probably means black. All these things are clear evidence of the non-Aryan origin of much that is in Śāktism.

Slater concentrates attention on South India. The two chief centres of Śākta worship, however, have been Rājputāna and Bengal. The Dravidians, though now confined mostly to the south, were formerly spread all over the country, and can be traced in the north and all the way down the east side of the peninsula. Their influence on Hindu culture has been most pervasive.[1] Nevertheless, in the case of Bengal it is with a Mongoloid, or perhaps better Dravido-Mongoloid, people that we are concerned. And it has been contended by many that Tāntric practices had their origin in Assam and Bengal, and spread thence across Northern India. Vincent Smith, for instance, says that Kāmarūpa, the ancient independent kingdom centred in the Assam valley, 'is a gate through which successive hordes of immigrants from the great hive of the Mongolian race in Western China have poured into the plains of India, and many of the resident tribes are still almost pure Mongolians. The religion of such tribes is of more than local concern, because it supplies the clue to the strange Tāntric development of both Buddhism and Hinduism, which are so characteristic of mediæval and modern Bengal.'[2]

On Nilāchal hill, near Prāgyotishpur (now Gauhāti), stands the famous temple of Kāmākshā Devī, supposed to mark the spot where the generative organs of Satī fell, when her body was hewed in pieces by Vishṇu. It has been urged that here the Tāntric form of Hinduism came into being, and that from here it spread about the fifth century A.D.[3] From early times Kāmarūpa is recognised in Sanskrit literature as connected with Śākta rites. There are several allusions to it in the *Chaṇḍīmāhātmya*, though the author's knowledge of Eastern India appears to be hazy. The account of the Chinese

[1] Cp. Govinda Das, *Hinduism*, p. 185.

[2] *EHI*, p. 384. Cp. Glasenapp, *Brahma und Buddha*, p. 152.

[3] Cp. Crooke, 'Hinduism,' *ERE*, VI, 705; Anderson, 'Assam,' *ERE*, II, 132; Eliot, *Hinduism and Buddhism*, II, 127, 278, etc.; Glasenapp, *HSI*, pp. 120, 121.

pilgrim Hiouen Tsang, at the end of the Gupta period, seems to imply that the king and upper classes were Tāntric Hindus, but that much of the superstition and magic of the humbler folk had not yet been received within the pale of Hinduism. Śaṅkara Deva, probably under the inspiration of Chaitanya, led a Vaishṇava reformation in the sixteenth century, but failed permanently to suppress Tāntric practices, though they were for a time checked. The *Yoginī Tantra* probably dates from about this time, and contains many references to Kāmarūpa and instructions for worship there. 'Kāmarūpa,' it is said, 'is known as Devī's *kshetra*, there is no other like it. Elsewhere Devī is insignificant; at Kāmarūpa she is in every house. He who has once at Kāmākhya done *pūjā* of Mahāmāyā, both gains his desires here, and hereafter the form of Vishṇu. There is none like him, and no other work of his is reckoned at all.'[1]

It is in Assam and Bengal that today the cult of Kālī appears in its most primitive forms among the wilder tribes. Tippera, for instance, is the scene of Tagore's play *Sacrifice*, in which Tāntric practices are referred to. Tagore's father, Devendranath, in his *Autobiography* describes how he came upon some Chittagong Bengalis who had carried an image of the Mother to a Burmese town, that they might celebrate Durgā *pūjā* while they were away from home trading.[2] In Bengal certain elements of the modern Nationalist movement have been linked closely with Śākta ideas. There are still country districts where it is held that the Tāntric deities prefer to be worshipped by the lower classes rather than by the Brāhmans. 'In many localities Durgā is worshipped first by the untouchable classes and then by Brāhmans. Brāhmans have to wait in some villages till the *pūjā* has commenced at some *Hāḍi's* house in the neighbourhood. The *Jayadratha Yāmala* says that the Devī likes to be worshipped by oil-pressers.'[3] In certain cults which include Buddhist as well as Tāntric elements, such as the worship of Śītalā Devī and Dharma worship, the priests are called *Dom Pundits*, which seems an

[1] Munro, *Macdonald MSS.*, Pt. II, p. 97; Farquhar, *ORLI*, p. 354. *Kshetra* = dwelling-place.

[2] op. cit., p. 185; cp. Crooke, 'Bengal,' *ERE*, II, p. 492.

[3] H. P. Śastri, *Modern Buddhism*, p. 12. *Yāmala* = a pair, the reference here being to a divinity and his *śakti*.

indication of their outcaste origin, for the Doms are the lowest menials of the plains.[1] Similarly in South India the ministrants at the worship of the village goddesses are often non-Brāhmans.

All this seems to supply *a* clue, though not *the* clue, as Vincent Smith suggests, to the developments we are considering. It is as unlikely that Śāktism originated in Assam, as that it is nothing but a Dravidian phenomenon. In all the centres of this worship in the different parts of India we see the same process at work. Local cults, often cults belonging to pre-Aryan India, and in some cases, perhaps, to pre-Dravidian India, have been admitted into Hinduism, have reacted upon one another, have been traced to a common source, have received philosophical justification and have been allegorised. Hinduism has been well described by Govinda Das as 'an anthropological process.'[2] This adoption and blending of cults has gone on simultaneously in many places, but for a variety of reasons it is to be seen most strikingly in Central India and in Bengal and Assam. Woodroffe's remarks on this point are worth quoting, for he so seldom considers Śāktism from the historical standpoint:

> Probably there were many Avaidika cults, not without a deep ancient wisdom of their own, that is, cults outside the Vaidik religion which in the course of time adopted certain Vaidik rites such as Homa; the Vaidikas in their own turn taking up some of the Avaidika practices. It may be that some Brāhmaṇas joined these so-called *Anārya-Sanpradāyas* just as we find today Brāhmaṇas officiating for low castes and being called by their name. At length the Shāstras of the two cults were given at least equal authority. The Vaidik practice then largely disappeared, surviving chiefly both in the Smārta rites of today and as embedded in the ritual of the Āgamas. These are speculations to which I do not definitely commit myself. They are merely suggestions which may be worth consideration when search is made for the origin of the Āgamas. If they be correct, then in this, as in other cases, the beliefs and practices of the soil have been upheld until today against the incoming cults of those Āryas who followed the Vaidik rites and who in their turn influenced the various religious communities without the Vaidik fold.[3]

'As in the case of Greece,' says Macnicol, 'so also here we must suppose the invasion of a lordlier culture by aboriginal

[1] Cp. D. C. Sen, *HBLL*, p. 31; Crooke, 'Doms,' *ERE*, IV.
[2] *Hinduism.* [3] *Shakti and Shākta*, p. 74.

races, "with their polygamy and polyandry, their agricultural rites, their sex emblems and fertility goddesses." '[1]

One further suggestion which has been made regarding the origin of Śāktism must be considered. There have been various discussions as to the connection between Tāntric Hinduism and Tāntric Buddhism. It is here that Eliot's distinction between Śāktism and Tāntrism is of value. He regards the latter as primarily a system of magic. In Hinduism it is inextricably linked with Śākta ideas, and even in Buddhism is very closely connected with the goddess-worship which established itself in the Mahāyāna system, but the two movements are in theory, if not in practice, separable. Śāktism and Tāntrism are two intersecting but not coinciding circles. The Tāntric forms of both Hinduism and Buddhism are in many respects very similar, and modern developments tend to blur the distinctions between them. Kālī, for example, has been adopted into the Mahāyāna Buddhism of Tibet by name.[2] Among the texts issued by Avalon is the *Śrīchakrasambhara Tantra*, the first Buddhist Tantra to be published, and the first to be translated into any European language';[3] it offers a strange medley of Buddhist and Hindu ideas.

Dr. Macnicol quotes, with apparent approval, the suggestion of H. P. Śastri, that it was by way of Buddhism that Tāntric practices gained a foothold in Hinduism. 'From being a worship followed by aborigines and outcastes, Tāntrism passed by the help of Buddhist prestige to take its place, in the twelfth or thirteenth century, among the higher classes.'[4] This seems to date its recognition too late, but we need to bear in mind that while Buddhism practically died in India after the Muhammadan attacks in the twelfth century, it lived on in Bengal and Orissa until the sixteenth. M. T. Kennedy, in his book on Chaitanya, speaks of 'Tāntric practices left behind

[1] *Indian Theism*, p. 181. The quotation is from Murray, *Four Stages of Greek Religion*, p. 78. In Greece the Northern conquering race effected a reformation in the beliefs and practices of the 'Age of Ignorance.'

[2] Cp. Crooke, 'Hinduism,' *ERE*, VI.

[3] *TT*, VII, p. iii.

[4] *Indian Theism*, p. 182. Cp. Śastri, *Modern Buddhism*, p. 27.

by Buddhism.'[1] On the other hand, Barth says that 'the obscenities of the Śivaite *Tantras* have deeply infected the Buddhist *Tantras* of Nepal . . . and through them the Tibetan translations, the majority of which are of a date prior to the ninth century.'[2] In the opinion of de la Vallée Poussin, 'Buddhist Tāntrism is practically Buddhist Hinduism, Hinduism or Śaivism in Buddhist garb.'[3] Basing himself on the work of Barth, H. Kern, and Poussin, Winternitz argues that from Bengal the *Tantras* penetrated to Nepal and Tibet, and caused there the growth of Tāntric works hardly distinguishable from those of the Indian Śāktas.[4] A similar view is taken by Sten Konow in the new edition of Chantepie de la Saussaye's *Lehrbuch*,[5] and by Eliot. It is confirmed by Heinrich Zimmer's examination of the *Śrīchakrasambhara Tantra*.[6]

It seems more likely that the movement was from Hinduism to Buddhism rather than from Buddhism to Hinduism, but in all probability the gradual recognition of popular cults, which has already been considered, went on within each religious system about the same time. No doubt each affected the other, but what was really happening over the whole area was the absorption and blending of primitive beliefs and practices. Avalon summarises an essay on *The Antiquity of Tantra*, by an Indian scholar, which deals incidentally with the suggestion that Tāntrism is derived from Mahāyāna Buddhism. Much that the author says is uncritical, but he is surely right in denying that 'similarity between two doctrines and practices is necessarily proof that the first is borrowed from the second.'[7] The study of comparative religion furnishes many examples of what has been called 'developmental coincidence.' At the end of a book of German translations of Sanskrit passages, Rudolf Otto prints a very interesting and important essay on *Das Gesetz der Parallelen*

[1] *The Chaitanya Movement*, p. 3.
[2] *Religions of India*, p. 201.
[3] 'Tantrism (Buddhist),' *ERE*, XII, 193.
[4] *Geschichte der indischen Literatur*, I, 482.
[5] op. cit., II, 129.
[6] *Kunstform und Yoga*, p. 67 f. Cp. Hauer, *Die Dhāraṇī*, p. 18.
[7] *Principles of Tantra*, Introduction, p. xxxvii f.

in der Religionsgeschichte, in which, after setting out in impressive fashion a number of parallels from different parts of the world, he urges that it is in most cases a mistake to talk of 'borrowing.' All we can truthfully speak of is 'convergence.' There seems to be a law of parallels in religious development.[1] Otto is dealing with the subject on a large scale, but many of the things which he says apply to narrower fields.

Authorities on Buddhism point out that many Tāntric rites are older than the time of the Buddha.[2] Śāktism, in the sense in which Eliot uses the word, 'erotic mysticism founded on the worship of goddesses,'[3] may be no earlier than the Christian era. It seems to have been about the eighth century that Tāntrism and Śāktism established themselves among Indian Buddhists. Similar ideas were then at work in all the Indian systems. Goddesses are praised in hymns and represented in temples which are Jain.[4] Even in some Vaishṇava sects, Śākta principles were at work.[5] There was everywhere the upward thrust of century-old beliefs and superstitions. The official religions of the day had failed to satisfy the needs of the ordinary man.

[1] *Vischnu-Narayāna*, p. 205 f.
[2] Cp. Poussin, *JRAS*, 1904, p. 557.
[3] *Hinduism and Buddhism*, II, p. 124.
[4] Cp. Glasenapp, *Der Jainismus*, Sections I and VI.
[5] Cp. Otto, *Vischnu-Narayāna*, pp. 157–59.

CHAPTER VII

THE SĀṄKHYA AND VEDĀNTA PHILOSOPHIES

It is time that due regard should be paid to the non-Aryan elements in Indian civilisation and religion. They are clearly to be seen in Śāktism. It must not, however, be forgotten that there were things even in the *Veda*, and certainly in the *Brāhmaṇas* and *Upanishads*, which made development along Śākta and Tāntric lines easy, particularly when such development was stimulated by the presence of popular cults demanding recognition. There was, as has already been pointed out, a darker side to Aryan religion. The difference between conquerors and conquered may not have been quite so great as has often been thought. More than that, there were intellectual and philosophical forms ready to receive and mould the new life from below.

Brian Hodgson, who lived in Kathmandu from 1820 to 1844, and drew attention to the special features of Nepalese Buddhism, spoke of Śāktism as 'lust, mummery, and black magic.' It is a phrase that has often been repeated, and to which Avalon vigorously and rightly objects. There is a very dark side to the movement, but at their best the *Tantras* are 'the repository of a high philosophic doctrine, and of means whereby its truth may, through bodily, psychic and spiritual development, be realised.'[1] Some Hindu scholars would have us believe that the grosser forms of Śāktism are perversions of an ancient and refined faith which owes nothing to lower cults, a faith in a goddess who can be as merciful as the Madonna of Christianity, and yet, since she is also the goddess of Nature, combines in herself both life and death. The history of Indian thought gives no support to such a

[1] *Principles of Tantra*, Pt. I, Preface, p. ix.

view. The allegorical and philosophical aspects of Śāktism are clearly later in time than its more primitive manifestations. Nevertheless, there were elements in ancient Indian thought which could easily provide a framework for Śākta ideas. Barth traced the roots of Śāktism 'far away in those ideas, as old as India herself, of a sexual dualism, placed at the beginning of things (in a *Brāhmaṇa* of the *Yajurveda*, for example, Prajāpati is androgynous), or of a common womb in which beings are formed, which is also their common tomb.'[1] Even if we regard the worship of goddesses, as at present practised, as of Dravidian and Mongolian rather than Aryan origin, we must admit that there is some truth in D. C. Sen's contention that 'when the Śākta cult came to be recognised by the Indo-Aryans, they raised it into a highly refined and spiritual faith, Sanskritised its vocabulary and Aryanised its modes of worship.'[2]

The philosophies underlying the *Tantras* are modifications of the Sāṅkhya and Vedānta systems.[3] The former may have been the earliest system of Indian philosophy and has obvious affinities with certain Śākta ideas. It began as a reaction from the idealistic monism of the *Upanishads*, and was possibly earlier than the time of the Buddha. Later it was adopted by the Brāhmans as one of the so-called 'orthodox' systems, and it flourished chiefly in those early centuries of the Christian era, when, as has already been noticed, Śākta ideas began to be prominent in the literature. The primary authority for the system, the *Sāṅkhya-kārikā*, a seventy-verse poem, is dated towards the beginning of the fourth century.

The Sāṅkhya (enumeration) system is usually described as an atheistic dualism. It is atheistic in the sense that it denies the existence of a supreme god; the popular polytheism was not attacked. It is dualistic since it maintains that there are two eternal existences—Matter (*prakṛiti*), which is one and productive, 'an eternal productive force or prolific germ,'[4] and, on the other hand, an infinite number of passive individual souls (*purusha*). 'The essential conception,' says

[1] *Religions of India*, p. 200. [2] *HBLL*, p. 251.

[3] Cp. S. Dasgupta, *History of Indian Philosophy*, I, p. 71; Sten Konow, *Lehrbuch der Religionsgeshichte*, II, 179.

[4] Monier Williams, *Brahmanism and Hinduism*, p. 183.

A. B. Keith, 'is that from unconscious nature there is developed for the sake of spirit a whole universe, that the development takes place for each individual spirit separately, but yet at the same time in such a manner that nature and its evolutes are common to all spirits.'[1] Although there is this idea of a necessary harmony between the worlds of the different individuals, the system is the reverse of that of Leibniz. For the European philosopher the individual is essentially active; according to Sāṅkhya thought he is in reality passive. Misery comes from the fact that the individual is led into imagining himself a thinking, feeling, willing, acting being. Deliverance comes through the recognition of the absolute difference between soul and matter, and the realisation that the ego has no real part in any movement, change, suffering or sorrow. 'The soul therefore abides eternally released from the delusion and suffering of this world, as a seer who no longer sees anything, a glass in which nothing is any longer reflected, as pure untroubled light by which nothing is illuminated.'[2]

In many Śākta works echoes of these ideas can be found. T. E. Slater, in his suggestive work on *The Higher Hinduism in Relation to Christianity*, says: 'The Tāntric idea of the production of the universe by the blending of the male and female principles—the quiescent and the active (*śakti*)—which lies at the root of the whole later mythology of India, owes its development to the popularisation of the Sāṅkhya philosophic idea of the union of the two principles Puruśa (soul of the universe) and Prakṛiti (the primordial essence and evolvent of all things).'[3] The energy of Vishṇu and Śiva was personified as a goddess and identified with *Prakṛiti*, the primary source of the universe. The connubial relations between Devī and her husband were held to typify the mystical union of the eternal principles, matter and spirit, which produces the world. The self-existent Being is regarded as single, solitary, impersonal, quiescent, inactive. Once it becomes conscious and personal it is duplex and acts

[1] *The Saṁkhya System*, p. 78.

[2] Oldenberg, *Buddha*, p. 67. Cp. Garbe, 'Sāṅkhya,' *ERE*, XI, p. 192.

op. cit., p. 5 n.

through an associated female principle, which is conceived as possessing a higher degree of activity and personality. *Śakti* is the instrumental cause, *Prakṛiti* the material cause, and Śiva the efficient cause of the world.[1]

Sāṅkhya thought was largely primitive, its forms being governed by the imagination. There was no ethical content to make it incompatible with the grossest conceptions of popular belief. In the *yoga* prescribed for the attainment of isolation (*kaivalya*) rationalism and superstition are combined. Salvation is offered to all four of the castes, and at first the school of *yoga* was open even to outcastes. The *Tantras* recognise no distinctions of caste or sex, and this provides another link with the Sāṅkhya system.

This dualistic philosophy, however, is less vigorous intellectually than Vedāntism, the philosophy of the *Upanishads*, which taught the identity of the universal and the individual *ātman*. There were many schools of Vedānta thought, modifications some in a more pantheistic and some in a more theistic direction. It is true to say that in some form or other it is the real philosophy of most Indians, and among those must be included many Śāktas. Woodroffe has suggested that Śākta teaching 'occupies in some sense a middle position between the dualism of the Sāṅkhya and Śaṅkara's ultra-monistic interpretation of the Vedānta.'[2] Śaṅkarāchārya, in commenting on the *Vedānta sūtras* of Bādarāyaṇa, which came from the fourth or fifth century, gave to them a strong monistic emphasis. The material world is regarded as pure illusion (*māyā*). The human soul is identical with Brahman, the Absolute. *Tat tvam asi*, 'Thou art that.' On the other hand, another school of commentators, probably less true to the original meaning of the *Upanishads* themselves than Śaṅkara, gave to the *sūtras* a more theistic meaning, and prepared the way for warm-hearted devotion to a personal god. The best-known philosopher of this *bhakti* school is Rāmānuja (*c.* 1100).

In the Śākta literature there are many traces of the different strands of Vedānta teaching, but the goddess seems

[1] Cp. Barth, *Religions of India*, p. 199.

[2] *SS*, p. 201. Cp. *ibid.*, pp. 9, 94 ff.; Glasenapp, *Brahma und Buddha*, p. 155.

always to be regarded in a more personal manner than is reconcilable with pure monism. In the poetry there are fine examples of *bhakti* piety, and occasionally even direct protests against the idea that personal identity will ultimately be lost. Rāmprasād cries:

What is the worth of salvation if it means absorption, the mixing of water with water! Sugar I love to eat, but I have no wish to become sugar.[1]

What the worshipper in general seeks is union with the Devī. In many places the *Tantras* teach that after the performance of the right ceremonies he actually becomes Devī. A few works like the *Prapañchasāra Tantra* and the *Śāradā-tilaka* are mainly Sāṅkhya in thought,[2] but the great majority are Vedānta in sympathy.

The more specifically religious interest must have helped the popularity of Śākta ideas. The old Vedic gods had declined in importance. Brahman had come to be the Unknown, the Impersonal, the Inert, a god of philosophy who could only be described by negatives.[3] Gradually Vishṇu and Śiva came into prominence, both of them supreme personal gods, more able to satisfy the needs of the human heart. But the theological defenders of these gods held that the highest condition of being is complete quiescence and inactivity, as well as complete oneness, solitariness and impersonality. Vishṇu, it is true, came near to men in his *avatāras*, his descents or incarnations. Śiva was often pictured as asleep; 'like a corpse,' according to one of the *Purāṇas*. His consort, therefore, came to be regarded as the personal deity in whom faith could rest. Devī was seen and near, and in addition to her terrifying aspects, there was, particularly in Bengal, a domestic and genial side, which made her worship 'religiously supremely attractive.'[4]

Nicol Macnicol has suggested that female deities are more capable than others of being identified with ideas, when early

[1] *BRLS*, XV, p. 40. The spirit of the poem is perhaps Vaishṇava rather than Śākta. But Rāmprasād is usually a theist.

[2] Cp. Avalon, *Principles of Tantra*, Pt. II, Preface, p. xv.

[3] Cp. Glasenapp, *Brahma und Buddha*, p. 123.

[4] D. C. Sen, *HBLL*, p. 251.

speculation is struggling to find some medium of expression. That may, perhaps, be so. He is certainly right in saying that Śāktism 'answers to many fears and passions that are deep in the human soul, and seem to be a part of the universe.'[1]

[1] *Indian Theism*, pp. 185, 187.

CHAPTER VIII

THE BACKGROUND IN BENGAL (A)

THE natural and historical background has not always been sufficiently taken into consideration in tracing the development of religious ideas. In the case of Śāktism its study proves particularly illuminating. The uncertainty of the divine is one of the notes most frequently struck. The priest in Rabindranath Tagore's play, *Sacrifice*, exclaims: 'Our Mother is all caprice. She knows no law. Our sorrows and joys are mere freaks of her mind.' A somewhat similar idea occurs in Śaṅkara's commentary on the *Vedānta sūtras*. Brahman, it is said, has neither desire nor love; how then should the world ever have been created? 'The activity of the Lord,' says Śaṅkara, 'may be supposed to be mere sport proceeding from its own nature, without reference to any purpose.'[1] How such a conception of the divine came to possess men will be better understood if conditions in Bengal are remembered. What Gilbert Murray tells us of Greece applies also to India.

The best seed-ground for superstition is a society in which the fortunes of men seem to bear practically no relation to their merits and efforts. A stable and well-governed society does tend, roughly speaking, to ensure that the Virtuous and Industrious Apprentice shall succeed in life, while the Wicked and Idle Apprentice fails. And in such a society people tend to lay stress on the reasonable and visible chains of causation. But in a country suffering from earthquakes, or pestilence, in a court governed by the whim of a despot, in a district which is habitually the seat of a war between alien armies, the ordinary virtues of diligence, honesty and kindliness seem to be of no avail. The only way to escape destruction is to win the favour of the prevailing powers, take the side of the strongest invader, flatter the despot, placate the Fate or Fortune or angry God that is sending the earthquake or the pestilence. The Hellenistic period pretty certainly

[1] II, 8, 32–33, *SBE*, XXXIV.

falls in some degree under all of these categories. And one result is the sudden and enormous spread of the worship of Fortune.[1]

The influence of geography on religion and politics is now realised. To the climate may be traced, in part at least, what a Westerner often regards as the too sensuous emphasis of the Indian. 'The physical facts of India, the blazing sun, the enervating rains, have coloured their mental outlook,' says the Montagu-Chelmsford Report.[2] Anderson traces the physical and moral decay produced in the fine manly Indo-Chinese invaders of Assam and Eastern Bengal to the soft, enervating and malarious conditions into which they came.[3] The peoples who entered India from Central Asia were similarly affected. The situation in rural Bengal has been thus graphically described by Edward Thompson:

> The peasant is fighting a losing battle. One year the heavens are shut and there is drought. The rivers are empty sands. Famine follows; and incalculable misery. The next year it rains in excess, and the vast watercourses swell with huge floods. The streams feel their way along their banks till they come to the sandhead which blocks an old course—Bengal is full of these 'blind rivers,' as they are called. Here the water checks a moment, like a darkened mind groping and feeling. Some dim memory stirs that once, it may be a century ago, the way was here; then the waters gather together and plunge through. A village, two miles from the main river, living in security all these years, beside its 'blind river,' will wake at midnight to find a shoreless sea heaving and thrusting at the mud walls. This experience may be repeated, not once, but often in one Rains, as if Nature were on ogress, watching till the folk had put together some makeshift shelter of palm-leaves and mud, to dash it to ground again. So the long, bitter fight goes on. The people, after centuries of this, have become patient, uncomplaining, hopeless. . . . But there come years when Nature seems caressing, indeed a Mother; when the rain is neither too much nor too little, but just sufficient. The fields are filled, the mud huts stand. It is not strange that Bengal should think of God as Mother; yet . . . should think of her with fear, as capricious and sometimes terribly cruel.[4]

'Nature,' says Bamfylde-Fuller, 'often appears to overhang humanity as a tormenting spirit. . . . Death steps alongside life. . . . Village life has its idyllic side; the promise of harvest is gilded by brilliant sunlight; in their cottages the poor have

[1] *Four Stages of Greek Religion*, pp. 112–14.
[2] Cp. Lovett, *Indian Nationalist Movement*, p. 19.
[3] Anderson, 'Assam,' *ERE*, II, p. 135.
[4] *BRLS*, pp. 15–16.

joys which are unknown in the slums and alleys of Europe. But Nature, which gives the increase, also appears to destroy it, and the deities that inspire her forces present themselves to the popular imagination in shapes that are cruel and repulsive.'[1] In a novel by Navin Chandra Sen, entitled *Bhānumati*, according to Anderson, 'the sense of the mingled horror and rapture of Śakti worship is expressed in a way that no mere description by a foreigner could convey,' and at the beginning reference is made to the cyclone and tidal wave which overwhelmed Chittagong in 1897.

The tale opens with a singularly beautiful and poetic description of the smiling aspect of the Chittagong coast in the late autumn, of the blue sea flecked with foam as the water of a lake is studded with swaying lilies, of the pale azure of the sky overhead, of the yellow sands shining in the happy brightness of morning sunshine and behind them the rich gold of ripening crops, varied by the dense green foliage, in which the brown-roofed cottages of the peasants nestle. To the north soars the sacred peak of Chandra-sekhar, crowned with the gleam of the white temple of the goddess, and to the south lies the rocky island shrine of the local Venus at Mashkal, an Indian Cyprus on a small scale. It is the eve of the annual festival at which, in old time, human sacrifices were offered to the goddess of life and death. The people are happy in the expectation of a plentiful harvest. They are preparing the simple presents with which they rejoice the hearts of their relatives and children; their minds are filled with gratitude for safety and prosperity, and sufficient food. But the goddess is bent on warning her creatures that death is her function as well as life and love and happiness. On the fated night of the cyclone, when the rough and simple peasant folk are quietly sleeping, the great wind blows suddenly without visible warning, and, catching up the rising tide, pours it in a torrent of impartial destruction over the sleeping coast, involving all—happy homes, men, women and children, ripening crops, prowling beasts of prey, and harmless domestic animals, even the birds of the air—in one common hecatomb. The goddess has exacted her own sacrifice, since men no longer offer victims at her altar.[2]

It is with such things in mind that Śākta beliefs must be studied.

[1] *Studies in Indian Life and Sentiment*, pp. 106–7.

[2] Anderson, 'Assam,' *ERE*, II, p. 134–35. The novel was issued in 1900. Cp. Pratt, *India and Its Faiths*, p. 65 n., for a reference to a cyclone in Telugu and a missionary's comment on it: 'I thought that our God means to show what He is able to do—to build up here among the heathen, and then how easily He can undo all.'

Equally important, however, is the relation of the history of the people to the rise and development of their religious ideas and customs. The study of a religion cannot rightly be separated from the general fortunes of the people concerned. Warde Fowler reminds us that 'an adequate knowledge of Roman history, with all its difficulties and doubts, is the only scientific basis for the study of Roman religion, just as an adequate knowledge of Jewish history is the only scientific basis for a study of Jewish religion. The same rule must hold good, in a greater or less degree, with all other forms of religion of the higher type, and even when we are dealing with the religious ideas of savage peoples it is well to bear it steadfastly in mind.'[1] In the case of Hinduism this advice is not easy to follow, for the course of Indian history is still at many points confused and uncertain. The main outlines do, however, throw considerable light on the growth of Śāktism. We shall confine our attention chiefly to Bengal.

The Indo-Aryan invaders worked their way only slowly across the Panjāb and down the courses of the Indus and the Ganges. Probably they advanced as far as the junction of the Jumna and the Ganges at a fairly early date, but Bihar and Bengal were long reckoned non-Aryan countries, while the peninsula to the south was hardly affected at all by the early Indo-Aryan movement. It has already been suggested that many of the characteristic Śākta practices and beliefs are traceable to the Dravidian and Mongolian peoples, and that they passed into Hinduism by a natural upward transition, as aboriginal, non-Aryan and casteless tribes adopted officially the religion of those immediately above them in the social scale. As Sir Alfred Lyall strikingly expresses it: 'The ethnical frontier,' described in the *Annals of Rural Bengal*, 'is an ever breaking shore of primitive beliefs, which tumble constantly into the ocean of Brāhmanism.'[2] We do not know enough of the early history to trace such changes in detail, but in more recent centuries, about which our information is fuller, it is possible to see a clear connection between

[1] *The Religious Experience of the Roman People*, p. 4.

[2] *Asiatic Studies*, pp. 102–3. The book referred to is that by W. W. Hunter.

economic, social and political conditions and the popularity of the Śākta cult.

It was in the confusion of the early centuries A.D. that the sect began to develop. By the time Harsha, who died about A.D. 647, was ruler of the empire, which included Bihar and the greater part of Bengal, the worship of Devī was recognised and taken for granted in the literature of the time. Radhakumud Mookerji has collected together the evidence for the state of religion and learning at the time, and also details about economic conditions and social life.[1] We learn much from the works of Bāṇabhaṭṭa, to which reference has already been made, and also from the account of his journeyings left by the Chinese pilgrim, Hiouen Tsang. Prolonged anarchy followed the decay of the Gupta power, and it was during these decades that Śāktism spread, and that many of its more objectionable features secured their hold. Farquhar, in his *Outline of the Religious Literature of India*, dates the main Tāntric movement in both Hinduism and Buddhism between A.D. 550 and 900. In order to introduce settled government in Bengal the people elected Gopāla, of the 'race of the sea,' as their king, and from him sprang the Pāla kings of Bengal, who maintained themselves in power for several centuries until the rise of the Senas, Brāhmans from the Deccan, who secured control of a part of the province early in the eleventh century, and continued their rule until the Muhammadan conquests, nearly two hundred years later. Throughout India Buddhism was 'slowly dying, poisoned by Tāntrism, and weakened by Hindu violence and criticism.'[2] From 700 to 1197 Bengal was remote from the main currents of Indian religion and from foreign raids. 'Little Aryan thought or learning leavened the local superstitions, which were infecting and stifling decadent Buddhism,'[3] says Eliot, and the same was true of Hinduism.

Bihar was captured by Muhammad Khiljī about 1197, and two years after Bengal was overrun with astonishing ease. It appears that the 'prevailing religion of Bihar at that time was a corrupt form of Buddhism, which had received liberal

[1] *Harsha.* [2] Farquhar, *ORLI*, p. 272.
[3] *Hinduism and Buddhism*, II, p. 127.

patronage from the kings of the Pāla dynasty for more than three centuries.' The fanatical Muslim warriors showed small respect for images, temples or worshippers, and 'after A.D. 1200 the traces of Buddhism in upper India are faint and obscure.'[1] A purely Muhammadan provincial administration was organised, and Bengal never escaped for any considerable time from the rule of the Muhammadans until they were superseded in the eighteenth century by the British. There was an attempt at rebellion in the thirteenth century, but it was probably a quarrel among Muslim chiefs rather than a rising of the populace. It was suppressed by the Sultan Balban (*d.* 1286) with great severity, and his family for the next fifty years held the governorship. Balban was merciless and cruel, but he did secure order; when he died 'all security of life and property was lost, and no one had any confidence in the stability of the kingdom.'[2]

Bengal soon became practically independent of the sultanate of Delhi, and for the next two centuries the history is one of wars, rebellions and assassinations. Once more it seems to have been times of uncertainty that saw Śākta ideas prominent. D. C. Sen tells us that Bengali literature begins about this time, and is full of the struggle between the worshippers of local goddesses who claimed to be *śakti* and more orthodox Hindus.[3] During the fourteenth century, in spite of the prevailing anarchy, Hindu literature was often encouraged by individual Muslim rulers. It contains frequent hints of the prevalence of Tāntric practices. The *Kālikā Tantra*, with its Blood Chapter, comes from the Bengal of this time. The fanatical Firoz Shah Tughlak, Sultan of Delhi from 1351 to 1388, boasts of how he dealt with an immoral sect whose beliefs seem to have resembled those of the more extreme Śāktas: 'I cut off the heads of the elders of this sect and banished the rest, so that their abominable practices were put an end to.'[4] The wish seems to have been father to the thought. Probably here, as at other times in the world's history, persecution increased the zeal and the numbers of the faithful. The life of the ordinary Bengal peasant must

[1] V. A. Smith, *OHI*, p. 221.
[2] Quoted by Smith, p. 228, apparently from Elphinstone.
[3] *HBLL*, p. 251. [4] Cp. V. A. Smith, *OHI*, p. 250.

have been a hopeless and helpless one, and it is not difficult to understand his seeking refuge in a conception of the divine as destruction, in a deity unreliable, irresponsible almost, dancing a mad dance of death, and propitiated only by cruel rites and degrading practices. In the cultus there was certainly degeneration, and at the end of the fifteenth century Hindus themselves reacted from the despondency and degradation connected with Śāktism.

The Vaishṇava revival, associated in Bengal with Chaitanya (1485–1533) and in Assam with Śaṅkara Deva (*c.* 1569), was due to a variety of causes, but it drew much of its strength from the reaction against Tāntrism. In Assam Śāktism seems to have been the religion of the Rājās, and Vaishṇavism spread as a democratic faith. In Bengal Chaitanya's was essentially a popular movement. M. T. Kennedy thus describes the situation:

> Irrespective of Brahmanic control, religious life was at a low ebb in Bengal at the time of Chaitanya's birth. The worship of deities hardly above the animistic stage was strongly entrenched in every village. Over these, following the priestly policy, had been loosely thrown the mantle of Hinduism. Cults of aboriginal origin, e.g. that of Manasā Devī (the serpent goddess), Dharma Thakkur, Ḍakshin Rai (the tiger god), Chaṇḍī and many others attached to the Śākta sect, were widely prevalent. The poison of Tantric practices left behind by Buddhism, and also deep set in current Hinduism, had gone far in the social order and exercised a peculiarly debasing influence on religious thought. The Śākta sect, which was probably the principle element in the Hinduism of that day, was neither a spiritual nor an æsthetic element in religion. Its annual sacrifice was a coarsening feature, while the Tantric strain of licentiousness in the theory and practice of its Vāmāchārī school gave it tremendous power for evil. If we may judge from contemporary works, the conditions of religious life were in sore need of reformation. To be sure most of these contemporary writers were Vaishṇava, and therefore liable to a charge of sectarian bias, but something more than a charge of partisanship is needed to explain away the volume and unanimity of references in the numerous Vaishṇava works of the sixteenth century to the widespread evil aspects of religious worship and practice in their day.[1]

During the period following the death of Chaitanya Bengal was the scene of animated disputes between Śāktas and Vaishṇavas. D. C. Sen gives the following picture:

[1] *The Chaitanya Movement*, p. 3.

The Vaishṇavas would not name the Java flower because it was the favourite of Kālī, the goddess of the Śāktas. They called it '*od.*' The word Kālī, which also means ink, they would not use, as it was the name of the goddess; they coined the word '*sahai*' to signify ink. The Śāktas, on the other hand, would vilify the Vaishṇavas by all the means that lay in their power. Narottama Vilas has a passage describing how the Śāktas went to Kālī's temple and prayed that she might kill the followers of Chaitanya Deva that very night. When the great Narottama Das died a body of Śāktas followed his bier, clapping and hissing as a sign of contempt for the illustrious dead.[1]

Chaitanya himself was an ascetic, and many of his companions held very strict views. Discipline was, however, relaxed after the death of the leader, and into the orders of ascetics there flocked thousands of converts from the degraded Śākta Buddhist orders, which were then passing through the last stages of decay in Bengal. Even in Vaishṇava circles, therefore, great impurity soon prevailed, and a most unhealthy eroticism.

Meantime important changes were taking place among the Muhammadans. Bābur of Kābul entered India in 1525, and, capturing Delhi and Agra, laid the foundations of the Mogul Empire. His grandson Akbar was enthroned in 1556, although then only fourteen years old, and after a year or two of petticoat government showed himself an ambitious and capable ruler, 'one of the most enigmatic figures in history, with much of the impellingly impersonal quality of Napoleon.'[2] Having secured his own position he proceeded to extend his dominions. Rājputāna was captured, then Gujarāt, then Bengal (1574–76), and finally Orissa, and certain lands on the north-west frontier. 'The territories under his rule,' says Vincent Smith, 'with their huge populations, fertile soil, numerous manufactures and vast commerce, both internal and sea-borne, constituted even then an empire richer probably than any in the world.'[3] Intellectually Akbar was a man of boundless curiosity and remarkable versatility. His religious history divides itself into three periods. Up till 1579 he was a convinced Sunni Musalman. From 1579 to 1582, after the issue of an 'Infallibility Decree,' which sought to make him Pope as well as Emperor, his belief in Islam gradually weakened, owing

[1] *HBLL*, p. 577. Java = Red hibiscus.
[2] Edward Thompson, *A History of India*, p. 35. [3] *OHI*, p. 311.

partly to contact with Hindus and Jesuit missionaries. In 1582 he tried to popularise a new religion to suit the whole empire, 'desiring that Hindus and Musalmans should worship in unison the one God, recognising the Pādshāh as His vice-regent on earth and the authorised exponent of His will.'[1] What he endeavoured to establish was something very like the Cæsar-worship of Imperial Rome. The Musalman chiefs of Bengal and Bihar rebelled in 1580, alarmed by his growing unorthodoxy and by his strict administrative measures. Fighting continued sporadically till 1612. It was during these years of rebellion and distress that the famous Śākta poet Mukundarāma flourished.

Mukundarāma is known among Indians as Kavikaṅkaṇ, 'gem of poets.' He has been compared by E. B. Cowell, who has translated into English a large part of his chief poem, *Chaṇḍī*, to William Crabbe,[2] but a closer parallel is furnished, as Edward Thompson suggests, by William Langland and his *Piers Plowman.*[3] The *Chaṇḍī-kāvya* was completed in 1589 and is a picture of the contemporary village life of Bengal. 'The poet,' says Rabindranath Tagore, 'was a poor man and was oppressed. So his only refuge was in the thought of this capricious Power, who might suddenly fling down the highest and exalt the lowest.'[4] The people were wretched and helpless, and the poet turned to Chaṇḍī, the powerful goddess in whom the dread energy of Śiva was active, and sought her aid. The poem re-tells the popular legends of Kālaketu the hunter, and of the merchant princes Dhanapati and Śrimanta, the latter connected with the temple of Kālī at Tamlūk,[5] but all through it is really the political state of Bengal that is depicted. A few years later, about 1600, another poet, Govinda Dās, gave one of the earliest metrical versions of a third popular story, that of Vidyā and Sundara, connected like the other two with Chaṇḍī, and later re-told by Rāmprasād and Bhārata Chandra Ray.[6]

[1] *Ibid.*, p. 369. [2] *JASB*, December, 1902. [3] *BRLS*, p. 13.
[4] Conversation quoted by Thompson, *BRLS*, p. 14.
[5] Cp. D. C. Sen, *HBLL*, pp. 298–303; Glasenapp, *HSI*, p. 117.
[6] Cp. *HBLL*, pp. 637–53; Thompson, *BRLS*, pp. 18–19; Glasenapp, *Der Hinduismus*, p. 396, gives a German translation of a few lines from Govinda Dās' *Kālikā-mangala*.

It was in 1565 that, under the influence of Śaṅkara Deva, Nara Nārāyaṇa (*d.* 1584), one of the greatest of the Koch rulers, sharing the Assam valley with the Āhōm kings, rebuilt the temple of Kāmākshā, which had been destroyed by the Muslims. Brāhmans were secured from Bengal for the opening ceremonies, in the course of which one hundred and forty men are said to have been sacrificed to the goddess.[1]

The age of Akbar is made the background of an important novel by Bankim Chatterji, entitled *Kapālakuṇḍalā.* In it several Śākta practices are described, and it gives a vivid picture of the life of the time. Shāhjahān, the grandson of Akbar, who was emperor from 1627 to 1658, a cruel and unscrupulous ruler, ordered the expulsion of the Portuguese from Hugli, where they had been established for more than fifty years, and fiercely persecuted the Christians they had made in the district. It is only fair to admit that the Portuguese had not been above using force to secure converts. Shāhjahān also directed his zeal against Hindus, and gave orders that 'at Benares, and throughout all his dominions in every place, all temples that had been begun should be cast down. It was now reported from the province of Allahabad that seventy-six temples had been destroyed in the district of Benares.'[2] In spite of these things, however, François Bernier, the learned French physician, who travelled and resided in the empire at the close of Shāhjahān's reign, and gives a gloomy impression of many parts, was enthusiastic in his account of the prosperity and orderliness of Bengal. He found supplies plentiful and remarkably cheap, and trade astonishing in its extent. 'In a word, Bengal abounds with every necessary of life,' he says, and quotes 'a proverb in common use among Portuguese, English and Dutch, that the kingdom of Bengale has a hundred gates open for entrance, but not one for departure.'[3] It may be mere coincidence that we possess no Śākta works which are dated in the first half of the seventeenth century, or it may be an indication that in the more ordered and prosperous times Tāntrism declined in importance.

[1] Cp. Gait, *History of Assam*, p. 56 f.; Anderson, 'Assam,' *ERE*, II, p. 134; Glasenapp, *HSI*, p. 120.

[2] Cp. V. A. Smith, *OHI*, p. 397.

[3] *Ibid.*, p. 418.

In another part of India, however, Śākta ideas were proving very influential, and in a manner which has had important consequences in Bengal in more recent times. A war of succession in Bījāpur, in the Deccan, enabled the Mogul Emperor to intervene. The imperial forces were, however, checked by the daring raids of the Marāthā leader, named Śivājī, who with the help of the Māwalis of the Western Ghats had gained control of a large tract of territory and had defeated the Bījāpur authorities. Aurungzēb, third son and successor of Shāhjahān, and two of his generals failed to suppress 'the Mountain-rat,' who in 1664 plundered the rich port of Surat with ruthless cruelty. Three years later the Emperor was persuaded to grant him the title of Rājā, but active hostilities were soon resumed, and the Marāthās met with further successes. In 1674 Śivājī proclaimed himself an independent king, and soon after led a daring expedition as far south as the Tanjore principality. The victorious chieftain died in his fifty-third year, in 1680. The Marāthā people do not play a conspicuous part in the early history of India, but Elphinstone says: 'A Rājpūt warrior, as long as he does not dishonour his race, seems almost indifferent to the result of any contest he is engaged in. A Marāthā thinks of nothing but the result, and cares little for the means, if he can attain his object. . . . The Rājpūt is the most worthy antagonist—the Marāthā the most formidable enemy.'[1] Both Rājpūt and Marāthā were united in their devotion to a goddess.[2] Śivājī lived on terms of intimacy with the *bhakta* poets Rāmdās and Tukārām, and was deeply influenced by them, but he worshipped Devī and believed that she sanctioned the execution of enemies even by treacherous means. Vincent Smith observes: 'The power of Śivājī over his people rested at least as much on his intense devotion to the cause of Hinduism as on his skill in the special kind of warfare which he affected, or on his capacity for organisation. Indeed, it is safe to affirm that his religious zeal was the most potent factor in arousing the sentiment of nationality which inspired his lowly country-

[1] Cp. *OHI*, p. 431.

[2] On Śākta worship among the Rājpūts see Tod, *Annals and Antiquities of Rajasthan*. Cp. Thompson, 'The Queen of Ruin' (in *Three Eastern Plays*) and *Kṛishṇa Kumari*.

men to defy the Mogul legions.'[1] It is on this combination of nationalism and devotion to Devī that a later generation in Bengal has seized.

Bengal continued in the hands of Muhammadan governors who made themselves more or less independent of the central authority. The lot of the average man became once more an unhappy one. There were raids by the Āhōms of Assam, among whom Śāktism had reasserted itself. Conditions throughout the empire as a whole became worse and worse. The pictures given by Vincent Smith and D. C. Sen are not attractive ones. 'During the anarchical period which intervened between the death of Aurungzēb and the establishment of the British supremacy, the character of the princes and other public men of India had sunk to an extremely low level. Nearly all the notable men of that age lived vicious lives, stained by gross sensuality, ruthless cruelty and insatiable greed.'[2] 'Robbers and bandits overran the country; and knavery of all sorts was practised in the courts of the Rājās.'[3] 'In Bengal the village communities, which still held rural society together in upper India, dissolved, and the *kānūngōs* ceased to maintain their records properly. Individual zemindars, originally mere collecting removable middlemen, developed into hereditary potentates, each controlling a huge extent of country. The Mogul government always had been in the habit of allowing local landholders and middlemen, whatever their designation might be, to exercise practically despotic authority over the peasantry.'[4]

The eighteenth century, as will be seen in greater detail in the next chapter, witnessed a revival of Śāktism. New *Tantras* appeared, and in Bengal there was a remarkable outburst of Śākta poetry.

[1] *OHI*, p. 432; Farquhar, *ORLI*, p. 356. [2] *OHI*, p. 487.
[3] *HBLL*, p. 615.
[4] *OHI*, pp. 563–64. The *kānūngōs* were hereditary skilled officers, who made assessment as to the share of produce to be paid to the government by the tenants.

CHAPTER IX

THE BACKGROUND IN BENGAL (B)

In the first half of the eighteenth century Bengal was plundered by the Marāthās; then, after the Nawāb Sirāj-ud-daula had seized the English factory near Murshidābād, and had captured Calcutta (an event always associated in English minds with the 'Black Hole' incident of 1756), the province was invaded by Clive, who by guile and skill was soon its master. In the following years it became the centre from which British supremacy spread. Even under a governor like Warren Hastings (1772–74), however, the condition of the ordinary inhabitants must have been a desperate one. Dacoits or brigand gangs committed terrible depredations. Even more formidable were the ravages of the *Sanyāsīs*, fanatical Hindu banditti. Hastings put down brigandage by hanging offenders in their own villages, breaking up their families and selling them as slaves, and fining the local community as accessory to the crime. The Penal Codes of Europe at the time were ferocious in their cruelty. To add to the miseries of Bengal, there was in 1770 a disastrous famine, due to the early cessation of the rains in the previous year. It is estimated that over a third of the population perished. Hunter, in his *Annals of Rural Bengal*, gives a vivid description by an eyewitness, and comments that the famine furnishes 'the key to the history of Bengal during the succeeding forty years.'[1] In spite of the appalling distress, the deputy of the titular Nawāb collected the revenue almost in full, and in 1771 demanded an additional 10 per cent. In his report to the East India Company Directors for the next year, Warren Hastings reported that

[1] op. cit., p. 19. Cp. B. C. Chatterji, *Ānanda Maṭh*.

the total amount had been 'violently kept up to its former standard.'[1]

It was in such circumstances that Śāktism became once more a power. Bhāskararāya (or Bhāskarānandanatha), a well-known commentator on some of the earlier *Tantras*, lived in the first decades of the century as court pundit in Tanjore.[2] In Bengal new *Tantras* were produced. Govinda Das speaks of the *Meru Tantra* as one of the best known Śākta works, and since it mentions the English it cannot be earlier than the eighteenth century.[3] More important were the famous *Mahānirvāṇa Tantra* and the *Tantrasāra*, which come from about this time. It was also an age of Śākta poets, chief among them being Rām Prasād Sen (1718–75) and Bhārata Chandra Ray (1722–60). Bengali literature was not without faithful patrons at certain of the local courts, but a rigid classical and artificial style had developed. There was revolt from what D. C. Sen calls 'the high-strung idealistic spirituality'[4] of Vaishṇava literature, and men revelled in grossly sensual ideas.

It is proof of the greatness of Rām Prasād, that in spite of the literary traditions of the time, and even in translation, one feels pulsing through his lyrics the earnestness of their author. Rām Prasād wrote an unsuccessful version of the Vidyā-Sundara story. His failure is no real discredit to him, for the elaborate poem on the same subject, by Bhārata Chandra Ray, the *Ānanda Mangala*, could only have been written in an age whose moral tone had become vitiated. 'In Bhārat Chandra,' says D. C. Sen, 'his inimitably finished style, and classical dignity of words, and their wealth of music invest even the most erotic matters with a literary fineness which, to some extent, hides the nudity of the disgusting scene. Many of his imitators, however, without possessing the grace and scholarship of the great master, imbibed his faults to a point outrageous of decency.'[5] The host of poets who imitated the style of Bhārata Chandra Ray, and wrote in the latter part of the eighteenth century, pro-

[1] Cp. V. A. Smith, *OHI*, p. 508.
[2] Cp. Farquhar, *ORLI*, pp. 192, 358.
[3] *Hinduism*, p. 127. Cp. Avalon, *Principles of Tantra*, p. lx.
[4] *HBLL*, p. 621. [5] *Eastern Bengal Ballads*, II, 1, p. 330.

duced works which have now been suppressed by the Indian Penal Code. It is different with Rām Prasād. The spirituality of the man, his genuineness, and his sincerity continue to make their appeal, and his songs are still known and loved all over Bengal. Sister Nivedita tells us that they were often on the lips of Swami Vivekānanda. There are many echoes of them in the poems of Rabindranath Tagore.

Rām Prasād's lyrics are sometimes delicate and haunting, sometimes 'a clashing of puns on Kālī's names, something that sounds (and is) very like a Bengali version of 'Peter Piper picked a peck of pickled pepper.'[1] The poet pours into Devī's ears the story of his woes, and begs her to release him from the prison-house of the world. She is his mother. He does not hesitate with childish petulance to reproach her for treating him as an enemy rather than as a son, and for turning a deaf ear to his prayers. At times he threatens he will no longer call her mother. At other times he says he is like a child chastised by his mother, but in spite of it only clinging to her the closer, crying, 'Mother, Mother.' In other moods he celebrates Kālī the Battle-queen. There is in the poems, as Sutton Page reminds us, much of the mingled protest and submission of the *Book of Job*, protest against unmerited suffering, submission to the inscrutable divine decrees.[2] It is this note which partly explains the hold they have had over the patient and long-suffering peasantry of Bengal, whose hard lot they depict with much feeling and faithfulness. In his attitude to sacrifices, the poet reminds us of the eighth century prophets of Israel. His is an intense personal religion. The cry, 'If I forget you, I endure the burden of the grief that burns,' seems to come from a heart which would have understood what Jeremiah meant when he said: 'If I say I will not make mention of Him . . . then there is in my heart as it were a burning fire shut up in my bones.'[3]

One or two examples of his songs may be given. The first is the voice of a man entangled in life's duties and difficulties, and wishing he could escape to give himself to the service of God.

[1] Edward Thompson, *Tagore, Poet and Dramatist*, p. 289.
[2] *International Review of Missions*, XIII, p. 617.
[3] *BRLS*, p. 35. Cp. Jeremiah, XX, 9.

In what have I offended so?

Unendurable has my daily lot become, all day I sit and weep. Inwardly I say, I will leave my home, I will dwell no longer in such a land. But the Wheel of Life turns me in its circle, and Chintārām *Chāprāsi* awaits me. I say I will leave my home, and pass my days praising the Name. But you, Kālī, have so wrought that I am bound fast to this vain show of things.

Weeping at Kālī's feet, poor Rām Prasād says: This Kālī of mine, this Kālī of my thought, through her I have become wretched.[1]

A second illustration of his rejection of the current attitude to pilgrimages and ceremonies is furnished by the following:

What have I to do with Kāśī? The Lotus-Feet of Kālī are places of pilgrimage enough for me. Deep in my heart's lily, meditating on them, I float in an ocean of bliss. In Kālī's name where is there place for sin? . . .

The worshipper laughs at the name of Gayā, and at ancestral offerings there, and the story of salvation by ancestors' merits. Certainly Śiva has said that if a man dies at Kāśī he wins salvation. But devotion is the root of everything and salvation but her handmaid who follows her. What is the worth of salvation if it means absorption, the mixing of water with water? Sugar I love to eat, but I have no wish to become sugar.

Prasād says joyously: By the power of grace and mercy, if we but think on the Wild-locked Goddess, the Four Goods become ours.[2]

Many of his poems deal with the problem of death and the hereafter. This one has haunted Rabindranath Tagore and phrases from it occur in his songs:

My play is finished, Mother. My play is finished, thou Joyous One. It was to play that I came to the earth, I have taken its dust and played. O thou Daughter of the Mountains, now am I in fear of death, for death is close at hand. In childhood's days what games I had! Then I wasted in the joys of married life the breath that should have been given to prayer.

Rām Prasād says: 'Now that I am old and feeble, tell me, Mother, what I must do. O Mother mine, thou that art strength itself, give me devotion. Cast me into the waters of salvation.[3]

The poet began life as a copyist in an estate office, but later found favour at the court of the Rājās of Kṛishṇagar.

[1] *BRLS*, No. IX. Chintārām (Lord of Anxiety) is Death, and is pictured as waiting like a *Chāprāsi* (Servant in Livery) to tell the man he is wanted elsewhere.

[2] *BRLS*, No. XV. The Four Goods are religious merit, wealth, physical desire, and liberation of the spirit.

[3] *BRLS*, No LXI.

Many stories have gathered round his life, some of which may be read in Edward Thompson's introduction to the translations of his lyrics, and in the pages of D. C. Sen. He was a Śākta, but not a Tāntric, in the sense in which Eliot uses these terms. When we remember the times in which he lived it is not difficult to understand why he was a devout worshipper of the goddess Kālī. It is easier to call God all-merciful, kind and benign in a well-ordered civilisation than in the midst of anarchy and distress. In such circumstances it is not so much the tender aspects of the deity, but the awe-inspiring, the dark and the terrible, which confront men at every step, and cannot be ignored or easily explained away. The Creator is seen also as the Destroyer. The Śāktas recognise these things, and in the words of D. C. Sen, 'a sweet and complete resignation of oneself to the Divine Power, knowing it to be terrible, makes the devotee, according to them, grapple better with the problems of life, from a spiritual point of view.'[1] Swami Vivekānanda used to say that the object of his worship was 'Kālī with her foot on the heart of her worshipper.'[2] On its less reputable side we have seen how much there is in Śāktism that is revolting and the reverse of spiritual, and it is significant, as Eliot points out, that 'Rām Prasād makes the worship tolerable because he throws aside all the magic and ritual of the *Tantras* and deals straight with what are for him elemental and emotional facts.'[3] 'Through the fierce and terrible he sees the sweet moonlight of grace that suddenly breaks forth, and Kālī is no more than a symbol to him—a symbol of divine punishment, of divine grace, and of divine motherhood.'[4]

There were other Śākta poets, many of them strongly influenced by Rām Prasād, such as Kamalākānta Bhattāchārya (*c.* 1800) and Dāśarathī Rāy (1804–57). The nineteenth century, however, saw a great improvement in the condition of Bengal. Law and order were established. Commerce developed. It became the policy of the East India Company to foster Western education, which had been begun by

[1] *HBLL*, p. 713.
[2] Cp. Sister Nivedita, *The Master as I Knew Him.*
[3] *Hinduism and Buddhism*, II, p. 288.
[4] D. C. Sen, *HBLL*, p. 714.

Christian missionaries and by other Europeans and Hindus. Famine relief was organised. Some of the grosser abuses tolerated generally by Hinduism, though at different times individual Hindus had protested against them, were suppressed. When in 1829 Sir William Bentinck declared *sati* illegal, although instances of it had been extremely numerous during the preceding quarter of a century, there was not such a general outcry as might have been expected.[1] Many Hindus approved the prohibition of human sacrifice in 1835, and the suppression of the Thugs. Farquhar, in his book *Modern Religious Movements in India*, traces the new life which welled up from within Hinduism early in the nineteenth century. The movements were largely of Western inspiration. The Brahma Samāj grew out of an unofficial gathering of theists, influenced by Rām Mohan Ray (1772–1833), 'a Brāhman whose abilities and character place him among the three or four most admirable Indians that ever lived.'[2] Reform societies grew up among Muhammadans.

All these things led to the condemnation of many Śākta practices. Śākta ideas made less appeal to men. But though to belong to it became either less distinctive or less respectable, the sect continued, and was not without influence. The rich and orthodox family of Tagore, though in some ways liberal, clung devoutly to the worship of Kālī, and the use of her images. Devendranath Tagore (1818–1905), whom Friedrich Heiler speaks of as 'without doubt the greatest religious personality of the nineteenth century India,'[3] broke away from his relatives in these respects, yet one of the finest hymns he used in Brahma Samāj services was adapted from the *Mahānirvāṇa Tantra*.[4] The mystic Rāmakṛishṇa, as has already been pointed out, remained throughout his life under the influence of Śākta ideas, and interpreted much of the traditional language regarding the Devī extremely literally. His influence is traceable on Keshub Chunder Sen, the Swami Vivekānanda, and on Brahmabandhav Upadhyaya. All of these were under more or less strong Christian

[1] Cp. Thompson, *Suttee*; and Lovett, *Asiatic Review*, April, 1928.
[2] Thompson, *A History of India*, p. 64.
[3] *Christliche Glaube und indische Geistesleben*, p. 11.
[4] Cp. *Autobiography*, p. 87 f.

influence, and yet remained apologists for the worship of the goddess.

The attitude of these leading religious personalities has to be understood in the light of the definite reaction against the liberalising and Westernising tendencies which showed itself at the end of the century. That all was not well had been shown by the Mutiny in 1857, which, though it may have been primarily 'a military mutiny of the Bengal army,'[1] was also in some places a popular revolt against British supremacy and British Christianity. Atrocities on both sides left lingering and bitter memories.[2] In Bengal itself there had been few disturbances, yet the subsequent years were filled with disputes between European indigo-planters and the peasantry, which brought to light the sufferings of many of the latter. The Bengali drama by Dīna Bandhu Mitra (1829–73), *Nil Darpan*, or 'The Indigo Planting Mirror,' published in 1860, gives a realistic picture of the conditions about this time. The English translator was fined and imprisoned for libel.[3] A serious famine in Orissa in 1865, in which Bengal administration and the Government of India failed disastrously, was a reminder that Nature in its terrible aspects had still power. Relief organisations have been made steadily more efficient, but famine and disease continue to recur, causing widespread suffering.

Meanwhile orthodox Hinduism began to reassert itself, and among the educated classes a demand for self-government was heard. Farquhar dates the movements for the defence of the old religions, and the beginnings of political aspirations between the years 1870 and 1895. The enhanced cost of living put the heaviest burden on the clerk, the teacher, and the petty Government official, those most receptive to such ideas. With these things has gone another revival of the cult of Kālī. The case of Keshub Chunder Sen seens typical of the change that came over Indian thought about this time. His training and sympathies had been Vaishṇava. For long he had been a leading member of the

[1] V. A. Smith, *OHI*, p. 722.
[2] Cp. Edward Thompson, *The Other Side of the Medal*.
[3] Cp. V. A. Smith, *OHI*, pp. 669 n., 734; Frazer, *Literary History of India*, pp. 415–19.

Brahma Samāj, and much influenced by the figure of Jesus Christ. He had occasionally spoken of the Motherhood of God, but it had played no large part in his message. Just at the time he was the object of attack because of the marriage of his daughter to the young Mahārājā of Cooch Behar, a marriage which seemed inconsistent in itself and in its rites with his previous teaching, Keshub made the acquaintance of Rāmakṛishṇa, the doubtless sincere but certainly unbalanced devotee of the goddess. The proclamation of the 'New Dispensation' was decided on by Keshub; out of the Brahma Samāj was to come a great revival uniting all the religions of the world. Enthusiastic missionaries were sent out through Bengal and Bihar. They were sent out in October, 1879, 'when all Bengal was throbbing with the great excitement of the national festival of Durgā *pūjā*,' and the proclamation they carried with them was as follows:

> Go and proclaim me Mother of India (said the Lord to his disciples gathered round him). Many are ready to worship me as their father. But they know not I am their mother too, tender, indulgent, forbearing, forgiving, always ready to take back the penitent child. Ye shall go forth from city to city and from village to village singing my mercies, and proclaiming unto all men that I am India's Mother. Let your behaviour and conversation, preaching and singing, be such as may convince those amongst whom you go that you are intoxicated with my sweet dispensation and sweeter name. And may India, so convinced, come to me saying, Blessed be thy name, sweet Goddess! We have heard and seen the Supreme Mother's apostles.[1]

Only a week before his death, in 1884, although he was very ill, Keshub took part in the dedication of a new sanctuary and offered what has been described as a most moving prayer to the Divine Mother.

Sister Nivedita dates Swami Vivekānanda's emphasis on the Mother from the summer of 1898, following a visit to a shrine in Kashmir. He himself spoke of a six years' inward struggle before he would accept Her.[2]

The partition of Bengal in 1905, and the agitation which continued till its modification in 1911, helped Śākta ideas once more to secure firm hold on the popular imagination. Kālī was regarded as a personification of the province.

[1] P. C. Mozoomdar, *Life and Teachings of Keshub Chunder Sen*, p. 362. [2] *The Master as I Saw Him*, pp. 162, 214.

Inspiration was drawn by the extremer nationalists from the life of Śivājī, both as regards spirit and method. Resistance to the British government received a religious sanction. Until late last century Śivājī had been almost entirely forgotten, and his tomb allowed to fall into ruin. The revival of his memory, and the conversion of it into a living force, is ascribed by Valentine Chirol, in his book *Indian Unrest*, to B. G. Tilak. Surendranath Banerjea made Śivājī a power in Bengal, and this was no small feat, since, for generations following the Marāthā raids, his name had been a bogey with which mothers hushed their babies. A new sense of helplessness, wretchedness and bitterness has again come over large sections of the population. Advanced political propaganda and agitation have been bound up in certain cases with a Śākta revival. In 1918 the Rowlatt Commission reported that the revolutionary outrages in Bengal were 'the outcome of a widespread but essentially single movement of perverted religion and equally perverted patriotism.'[1] The truth of the adjective 'perverted' may be disputed by some, but there can be no doubt as to the intimate connection here, as elsewhere, between religion and patriotism.

That the connection in many cases amounts to confusion is illustrated by the hymn *Bande Mātaram*, or 'Bow to the Mother,' which became a sort of Marseillaise of those opposing the partition of Bengal, and which has maintained its popularity in Nationalist circles. When the Indian National Congress met in Calcutta, in 1906, agitation was at its height, and Rabindranath Tagore attended, and sang this song to music he had himself written.[2] It comes from *Ānanda Maṭh* (The Monastery of Joy), the novel by Bankim Chatterji, which is based on the story of the incursion of the *Sanyāsīs* into Bengal during the governorship of Warren Hastings. These ascetics, well armed and disciplined, wandered about the province, their ranks swollen by a crowd of starving peasants, and obtained temporary successes against some Government

[1] Cp. Ronaldshay, *Heart of Aryavarta*, p. 80.

[2] Cp. Thompson, *Tagore, Poet and Dramatist*, pp. 102, 213–14. But when Tagore was asked to write a poem to Bengal as Kālī he refused, and prefers to personify the province as Lakshmī. Cp. *Letters to a Friend*, e.g. p. 42.

levies under British officers. The novelist puts into the mouth of the leader the following song:

I hail the Mother,
Well-watered, fruitful,
Dusky with crops,
The Mother!
With her nights made glad by brilliant moonlight,
Adorned with many trees with flowering blossoms,
With her pleasant smile and sweet speech,
Joy-giver, boon-giver,
The Mother!
O thou who art made fearsome by the hum of seventy million voices,
Thou who art armed with sharp swords grasped by twice seventy million hands,
Why, O Mother, art thou weak, when thou hast such might?
To thee the mighty one
I bow, the deliverer,
The queller of foes,
The Mother.
Thou art wisdom, thou art virtue,
Thou art in my heart, thou art my life,
Thou art the very soul in my body.
In (power of) arm art thou *Śakti*,
In (tenderness of) heart art thou *Bhakti*.
Thy image would I build in every temple.
Thou art Durgā armed with her ten weapons;
Thou art Kamalā (Lakshmī) wandering midst the lotus blossoms;
And Vāṇī (Sarasvatī) the wisdom-giver.
To thee I bow.
I bow to the fair,
Spotless, peerless,
Well watered, fruitful
Mother!
I hail the Mother,
The dusky, simple,
Smiling, richly-decked
Land, my nurse,
My Mother![1]

It is by no means certain whether this hymn was intended by Chatterji to be addressed to the goddess Bengal or the

[1] For this translation from the Bengali I am extremely obliged to Mr. W. Sutton Page, of the London School of Oriental Studies. A more metrical version in German is given by Otto von Glasenapp, *Indische Gedichte aus vier Jahrtausenden*, p. 121. This is from the seventh edition of *Ānanda Maṭh*. Lovett, *Indian Nationalist Movement*, p. 62, gives a few lines of the song.

goddess Kālī. They were not identified in the eighteenth century, and hardly by 1860, when the novelist was writing. 'From the context of the novel,' says Lovett, 'it seems that the Sanyāsī's appeal was rather to his mother's land, the land of Mother Kālī, than to his motherland.'[1] Ronaldshay quotes from the introduction to the first edition of the novel, in which the author wrote: 'Revolutions are generally processes of self-torture, and rebels are suicides. The English have saved Bengal from anarchy. These truths are elucidated in this work.'[2] He assumes that Chatterji would not have approved the uses to which his book has been put, but the passage in question is probably an example of the sarcasm so common in Bengali literature. In any case, however, the transition is not a difficult one from worship of the goddess to worship of Bengal or India.[3] 'Wife and children and all else are Her,' says Woodroffe, 'and service of them is service of Her. It is the one Devī who appears in the form of all. Service of the Devī in any of her aspects is as much worship as are the traditional forms of ritual *Upāsanā*. This is not to say that these may, therefore, be neglected. India also is one of Her forms—a specific *śakti*, the Bhārata *śakti*.'[4] In 1906 the new government of East Bengal declared the shouting of *Bande Mātaram* in the streets to be illegal, but during the Great War, at a recruiting meeting in North Bengal, British officers stood up with the rest of the audience and sang it.

Valentine Chirol records, in *Indian Unrest*, how 'practices which an educated Hindu would have been at pains to explain away, if he had not frankly repudiated them thirty years ago, now find zealous apologists,'[5] and he refers particularly to the revival of Śāktism. Leaders like Surendranath Banerjea have encouraged the linking of *śakti* and Kālī-*pūjā* with meetings

[1] *Indian Nationalist Movement*, p. 62.

[2] *Heart of Aryavarta*, p. 106.

[3] Cp. the hymn by Tagore sung at the 20th Indian National Congress in 1911 (German trans. by Otto, *Vischnu Nārāyana*, pp. 80–81), and the poems of Dvijendralāl Rāy (1864–1913. German trans. by O. von Glasenapp, *Indische Gedichte*, pp. 123–32.)

[4] *SS*, p. 433.

[5] op. cit., p. 27. Cp. *International Review of Missions*, XVII, p. 35. The first concern of Hinduism is 'no longer to amend its ways, but to assert its claims.'

in favour of *swarāj* and *swadeśi.* An advanced monthly paper was issued, called *Bande Mātaram*, edited by Arabinda Ghose, 'whose fervid writings were steeped in idealism, and who did more than anyone to breathe into the sinister spectre of anarchy the vitalising influence of religion.'[1] Ronaldshay quotes from a pamphlet by Ghose called *Bhawani Mandir*, which starts by declaring that a temple is to be erected to Bhawānī in the Himālayas, and that the help of all her children is needed. Who is Bhawānī? He proceeds to say:

> In the unending revolutions of the world, as the wheel of the Eternal turns mightily in its courses, the Infinite Energy, which streams forth from the Eternal and sets the wheel to work, looms up in the vision of man in various aspects and infinite forms. Each aspect creates and marks an age. . . . This Infinite Energy is Bhawānī. She is also Durgā. She is Kālī, she is Rādhā the beloved, she is Lakshmī. She is our Mother and creatress of us all. In the present age the Mother is manifested as the Mother of Strength. . . . The deeper we look the more we shall be convinced that the one thing wanting which we must strive to acquire before all others is strength—strength physical, strength mental, strength moral, but above all strength spiritual, which is the one inexhaustible and imperishable source of all others.[2]

Not all appeals to the Mother have been on as high a level as this, which is reminiscent of the teaching of Nietzsche. In one of her forms Kālī is represented as holding in her hand her own severed head, whilst the blood gushing from her trunk flows into her mouth. It is known as the Chinnamastika figure. A picture of this was published, with a note to the effect that the great goddess symbolised the Motherland 'decapitated by the English, but nevertheless preserving her vitality unimpaired by drinking her own blood.'[3] A favourite euphemism applied to the killing of an Englishman is 'sacrificing a goat to Kālī,' and it has been maintained seriously that killing with such a motive is no murder. Valentine Chirol gives several extracts from the Bengal press in which the goddess and her worshippers are addressed. One such may be quoted:

[1] Ronaldshay, *Heart of Aryavarta*, p. 128.
[2] *Ibid.*, p. 128 f.
[3] Cp. Ward, *History, Literature*, etc., III, p. 96; Wilkins, *Hindu Mythology*, p. 264.

ŚĀKTA PILGRIMS BATHING AT KALIGHAT

PREPARING THE RECEPTACLE FOR THE *HOMA* FIRE, KALIGHAT TEMPLE

For what sins, O Mother Durgā, are thy sons thus dispirited, and their hearts crushed with injustice? The demons are in the ascendant, and constantly triumphing over godliness. Awake, O Mother, who tramplest on the demons! Thy helpless sons, lean for want of food, worn out in the struggle with the demons, are struck with terror at the way in which they are being ruled. Famine and plague and disease are rife, and unrighteousness triumphs. Awake, O goddess Durgā! I see the lightning flashing from the point of thy bow, the world quaking at thy frowns, and creation trembling under thy tread. Let a river of blood flow, overwhelming the hearts of the demons.[1]

Al. Carthill, in *The Lost Dominion*, gives a vivid, though very unsympathetic, account of the increased popularity of the worship of Devī in Bengal and elsewhere, of the clubs of initiates formed to do her service, and of the assassinations which resulted. At the Coronation Durbar, in 1911, the King-Emperor announced that Bengal proper would remain undivided for administrative purposes, and in subsequent years Śākta ideas became less prominent. There was greater economic prosperity. Political agitation was less violent. But there has been recrudescence of Śāktism in Bengal and throughout India since the Great War. It has been connected in certain places with renewed *swarāj* agitation and the bitterness aroused by the events at the Jallianwalabagh, Amritsar, in April, 1919. An appeal to the goddess Kālī has been found a useful means of exciting feeling. Bloodshed has been justified by Śākta teaching. It is necessary to make quite clear, however, that this linking of a violent Nationalism with fanatical sectarian zeal is found only among certain groups of people. The movement for self-government is a very widespread one, drawing together men of all sections of Indian life and thought. This is not the place to describe or appraise it. The object here is simply to draw attention to the fact that the assistance of Kālī is invoked in some parts of India for the national cause.

All this account of happenings in Bengal from the very earliest times suggests that there is an intimate connection between outward conditions of life and Śākta beliefs. The natural social and political environment seems to have determined the progress or decline of the sect. In

[1] From the *Khulnavasi*. Cp. Chirol, *Indian Unrest*, pp. 18–19.

times of peace and prosperity it begins to lose its hold, but calamity and unrest give it fresh strength. Śāktism feeds chiefly on pessimism and despair. The bitterness of helplessness has led to the adoration of conscienceless strength in other lands than Bengal. Edward Thompson ventures on a prophecy, though with an important qualification: 'There has come such an access of mental happiness and self-respect to the people that it is certain they will not again feel as despondent as the poet of *Chaṇḍī* did, with no hope but from the intervention of sudden, irresponsible power. At least it will be unreasonable if they do.'[1]

[1] *BRLS*, p. 14.

CHAPTER X

SOME KINDRED RELIGIOUS PHENOMENA (A)

MANY of the ideas and practices which go to make up the Śākta movement in Hinduism are universal religious pheno mena. They can be paralleled in other lands and in other systems of belief. Too often there has been insufficient recognition of this, and even when it has been admitted, it has been forgotten that, in both East and West, 'though the wand-bearers are many, the initiates are few.'[1] Writers have been guilty of the historic injustice of comparing the Bacchi of the West with the thyrsus-bearers of the East. Rarely has the contrary injustice been committed.

The recalling of certain kindred religious developments from other parts of the world may help to a better understanding both of the strength and weakness of Śāktism. How curiously similar were some of the aspects of early Greek religion has already been suggested by the quotations from Gilbert Murray's work. The consideration of the background in Bengal, and the *Tantras* themselves, show that the movement was not unlike, in certain of its features, apocalyptic Judaism. Neither these, nor the parallels about to be adduced, should be pressed too closely. Others might be suggested. They bear witness to how many-sided is Śāktism. They are evidence of developmental coincidence, or, as Rudolf Otto calls it, 'convergence,'[2] rather than of any direct contact or borrowing, though in a few cases the possibility of this must not be quite ruled out.

[1] Plato, *Phaedo*, 69 C.

[2] See his suggestive essay, *Das Gesetz der Parallelen in der Religionsgeschichte*. *Vischnu Nārāyana*, p. 205 f.

I. The Worship of the Numinous

Śāktism affords many illustrations of those elements in religious experience to which Otto has drawn attention in his important book, *Das Heilige*. He indeed refers directly to the Śāktas in two passages, and not only are these references illuminating, but his whole thesis indicates a more sympathetic approach to such religious phenomena than is usually made.

'Religion,' he points out, 'is not exclusively contained or exhaustively comprised in any series of rational assertions.' 'The holy in the fullest sense of the word is a combined, complex category, the combining elements being its rational and non-rational components.'[1] To the non-rational element Otto gives the name 'Numinous,' and argues that it can best be described as *Mysterium Tremendum*, the experience of which induces 'creature-feeling' in the subject, and which may be analysed into elements of Awe, Overpoweringness, Energy or Urgency, the Wholly Other, and also Fascination. This is not the place for a critical examination of Otto's whole theory of religious experience, but clearly all the elements just enumerated may be traced in the religion of the Śāktas, not only in the wild and horrible rites of the burial-ground, but also in the case of a Rām Prasād. Otto's illustrations of his thesis come from the whole field of comparative religion, and furnish many interesting points of contact with Indian beliefs. He points out that the elements which make up the adjective *Tremendum*, Awe, Overpoweringness and Energy, are present in the widespread idea of a mysterious *ira deorum*. In the *Old Testament*, for example, the Wrath or Anger of Yahweh is realistically pictured in a way that has little or no concern with moral qualities; it is something numinous, as is also, though in a lesser degree, the *New Testament* conception of the ὀργὴ θεοῦ. In the Indian pantheon, as Otto remarks, there are several deities who 'seem to be made up altogether out of such as *orgé*, and even the higher Indian gods of grace and pardon have frequently, beside their merciful, their wrath form.'[2]

There are noteworthy descriptive similarities between the Semitic and the Indian conceptions of this Wrath of God.

[1] *The Idea of the Holy*, pp. 4, 116. [2] *Ibid.*, p. 18.

The following passage on the triumph of Yahweh, which was written probably about the fifth century B.C., recalls many of the pictures of Kālī:

Who comes here, all crimsoned, his robes redder than the vintage?
Who is it, arrayed with splendour, striding in his strength, radiant with victory, a mighty champion?
Why so red your robes, stained like a vintager's?

All alone I trod the winepress, for no nation lent me aid;
So I trod the foe in fury, trampled them down in my anger;
'Twas their blood splashed my robes, till all my clothes are stained.
For I resolved upon a day of vengeance; the time to free my folk had come.
I looked, but there was none to help, I was amazed that there was none to aid;
So my own power gained me the victory, it was my passion bore me on,
As I trampled the nations in my wrath and smashed them in my fury,
Spilling their blood upon the earth. (Isaiah, LXIII, 1–6.)[1]

Many of the more classic descriptions of Kālī's fights with the demons have points of contact with language like this. We are reminded of the pictures of the wild dance of a goddess garlanded with freshly-severed heads. Similar imagery is found in more recent accounts of the Devī's future victory over her enemies, by whom very often the British are meant. Even Rām Prasād pictures Kālī as the battle-queen.

Ever art thou dancing in battle, Mother. Never was beauty like thine, as, with thy hair flowing about thee, thou dost ever dance, a naked warrior on the breast of Śiva.
Heads of thy sons, daily freshly killed, hang as a garland around thy neck. How is thy waist adorned with human hands! little children are thy ear-rings. Faultless are thy lovely lips; thy teeth are fair as the *kunda* in full bloom. Thy face is bright as the lotus-flower, and terrible is its constant smiling. Beautiful as the rain-clouds is thy form; all blood-stained are thy Feet.
Prasād says: My mind is as one that dances. No longer can my eyes behold such beauty.[2]

[1] The translation is by Moffatt, from a slightly emended text. A similar image occurs in Revelation, XIX, 15. On the date of the above passage and other critical problems, see Whitehouse, 'Isaiah' (*Century Bible*).

[2] *BRLS*, No. XXIV. This is the only Battle-queen lyric in the selection. This is, as Mr. Sutton Page points out to me, inadequate representation of a whole group of Bengali poems with a similar theme.

The element of Awe has tended to recede in Western Mysticism, and in Christian Mysticism generally, Otto suggests, but in the East it has developed into a 'Mysticism of Horror, such as we find in certain forms of Indian Mysticism, both Buddhist and Hindu—in *Bhagavadgītā*, Chap. II—in some forms of Śiva and Durgā worship, and in the horrible form of Tāntrism.'[1] On its higher side this may be illustrated by Swami Vivekānanda, who used to speak often of 'the worship of the Terrible.' 'How few have dared to worship Death or Kālī,' he once said. 'Let us worship Death! Let us embrace the Terrible, because it is terrible, not asking that it be toned down. Let us take misery for misery's sake!'

> I am not one of those
> Who put the garland of skulls round Thy neck,
> And then look back in terror
> And call Thee 'The Merciful'!
> The heart must become a burial-ground,
> Pride, selfishness, and desire all broken in the dust,
> Then, and then alone, will the Mother dance there.[2]

It is interesting to notice the development in regard to the Eumenides, or Erinyes, in Greek religion. Like most chthonic spirits, they appeared first in a dual aspect, one friendly and beneficent, the other dark and sinister. Later they were represented only in their more terrible forms. The beneficent functions were left out of account, and they became finally the *Furiæ* of the Romans.[3] Certain forms of Kālī and Durgā seem to have had a similar history.

Otto contends, however, that the *tremendum* elements, although they have been subdued, are not wholly absent even from Christian thought and experience. He quotes from the writings of Henry Suso (1300–66), St. John of the Cross (*d.* 1591), and especially from Jacob Boehme (1575-1624),[4] to show that the non-rationally dreadful, and even the demonic phase of the numinous, remains a living element in intense religious experience. Luther, indeed, could say of God:

[1] *Idea of the Holy*, p. 109.
[2] Sister Nivedita, *The Master as I Saw Him*, pp. 164 f., 223 f.
[3] Cp. *ERE*, V.
[4] Cp. *Idea of the Holy*, p. 109 f.

Yea, He is more terrible and frightful than the Devil. For He dealeth with us and bringeth us to ruin with power, smiteth and hammereth us and payeth no heed to us. . . .

In His majesty He is a consuming fire. . . .

For therefrom can no man refrain: if he thinketh on God aright, his heart in his body is struck with terror. . . . Yea, as soon as he heareth God named, he is filled with trepidation and fear.[1]

In an interesting footnote, Otto suggests that 'Lucifer is fury, the ὀργή, hypostatized, the *mysterium tremendum* cut loose from the other elements and intensified to *mysterium horrendum.*'[2] The Śāktism we have been studying has intensified the feeling of awe to that of dread and horror, but has not separated it from the other elements in the experience of the numinous, from the element of fascination, for example, from which come ideas of Love, Mercy, Pity and Comfort.

Consciousness of the numinous is awakened, expresses itself and spreads from one to another in various indirect ways.

One of the most primitive of these—which is later more and more felt to be inadequate, until it is finally altogether discarded as unworthy—is quite naturally the 'fearful' and horrible, and even at times the revolting and the loathsome. Inasmuch as the corresponding feelings are closely analogous to that of the *tremendum,* their outlets and means of expression may become indirect modes of expressing the specific 'numinous awe' that cannot be expressed directly. And so it comes about that the horrible and dreadful character of primitive images and pictures of the gods, which seems to us today frequently so repellent, has even yet among naïve and primitive natures—nay, occasionally even among ourselves—the effect of arousing genuine feelings of authentic religious awe. And vice versa, this awe operates as a supremely potent stimulus to express the element of terror in different forms of imaginative representation. The hard, stern and somewhat grim pictures of the Madonna in ancient Byzantine art attract the worship of many Catholics more than the tender charm of the Madonnas of Raphael. This trait is most signally evident in the case of certain figures of gods in the Indian pantheon. Durgā, the 'great Mother' of Bengal, whose worship can appear steeped in an atmosphere of profoundest devotional awe, is represented in the orthodox tradition with the visage of a fiend.[3]

[1] See *The Idea of the Holy,* p. 103. Cp. Heiler, *Sadhu Sundar Singh,* 4th German edition, p. 124. [2] op. cit., p. 110 n.

[3] *Ibid.,* p. 64. Cp. Oman, *Science, Religion and Reality,* p. 290 f.; Paul Tillich, *Das Dämonische, ein Beitrag zur Sinndeutung der Geschichte.*

But not only in the figure of its goddess does Śāktism evoke and express the feelings to which Otto here refers. Many of its rites, especially those celebrated at night in the cremation ground, though full of dread and horror, are intimately connected with the experience of the numinous and sacred.

The use of only half intelligible, or quite unintelligible, language in devotion is another method of causing and presenting numinous feeling. It is found in almost all the great religious systems, and produces an unquestionably real enhancement of the awe of most of the worshippers. Otto has a special appendix on what he calls 'original numinous sounds,' which are the instinctive expression of intense feeling of this kind, and yet often have no meaning in the ordinary sense.[1] The Indian sacred syllable OM is one of the best examples of what is meant. Many of the *mantras* and *bijas* to be found in the *Tantras* belong to the same class of sounds, and their continued use can be better appreciated from this standpoint. Before impatiently dismissing them as 'mummery' it is well to note their parallel in the special emotional value attaching to words like Hallelujah, Kyrie Eleison, Selah, etc., just because they are quite different from the ordinary language employed, and convey no clear meaning. The Latin in the service of the Mass is felt by the Catholic to be, not a necessary evil, but something especially holy, and it is the same with the Sanskrit of the Buddhist Mass of China and Japan, and indeed the use of Sanskrit words in the worship of many Asiatic peoples who can have no idea of its literal meaning. There was a 'language of the gods' in the ritual sacrifices described by Homer, and many other parallels might be cited. Sometimes attempts have been made to suggest a direct connection between the 'numinous sounds' of different religious systems. J. W. Hauer, in the monograph already referred to, *Die Dhāraṇī im nördlichen Buddhismus*, gives the results of a careful examination of the mystical syllables occurring in the *Prapañchasāra Tantra* and those found in the so-called *Mithras Liturgy* discovered by

[1] *Idea of the Holy*, p. 194.

Dieterich. There are similarities in the type of religion, which will be noted in the next chapter, but Hauer's linguistic conclusions are: 'Among the many mystical syllables and words in the *Liturgy of Mithra* I cannot discover a single one that can be even remotely derived from Sanskrit. Nor is there anywhere a trace of the very ancient Indian magic words OM, HUM, etc.; and, similarly, there is nowhere among the Indian *dhāraṇī*, as far as I can see, a Greek word.'[1] This use of strange words and syllables to induce and express numinous feeling seems natural to mankind everywhere. It is found in its most developed form in the half-revealed, half-concealed, esoteric elements in the Communion service of the Greek Church. When the matter is viewed in the widest light we see some justification for the remark made by Otto, that the older Lutheran ritual has more of the real 'spirit of worship' than most of the proposed modernisations.[2]

Among the factors influencing the development of Śāktism, we have noted the effect produced by Nature in certain of her moods. Storm and pestilence have naturally everywhere coloured men's conception of God, and often a deep consciousness of the numinous element in the universe has come in the presence of these things. The *Old Testament* abounds in illustrations. Thunder and lightning, whirlwind and hail, cause not so much fear as a deep religious awe in men's hearts. This whole attitude finds its noblest expression in the closing chapters of the Book of Job, where the element of the mysterious is displayed in rare purity and completeness. 'Revelation is a mystery,' said Bishop Butler, 'but so is nature.' Otto sets side by side with the speeches of Yahweh out of the whirlwind a German story by Max Eyth, in which the building of the great bridge over the estuary of the Ennobucht is described.

In spite of endless difficulties and gigantic obstacles the bridge is at length finished, and stands defying wind and waves. Then there comes a raging cyclone, and building and builder are swept into the deep. Utter meaninglessness seems to triumph over richest

[1] op. cit., p. 23.

[2] *Idea of the Holy*, p. 67; cp. Heiler, *Katholischer und Evangelischer Gottesdienst*.

significance, blind 'destiny' seems to stride on its way over prostrate virtue and merit. The narrator tells how he visits the scene of the tragedy and returns again:

'When we got to the end of the bridge, there was hardly a breath of wind; high above, the sky showed blue-green, and with an eerie brightness. Behind us, like a great open grave, lay the Ennobucht. The Lord of life and death hovered over the waters in silent majesty. We felt His presence, as one feels one's own hand. And the old man and I knelt down before the open grave and before Him.'

Why did they kneel? Why did they feel constrained to do so? One does not kneel before a cyclone or the blind forces of Nature, nor even before Omnipotence merely as such. But one does kneel before the wholly uncomprehended Mystery, revealed yet unrevealed, and one's soul is stilled by feeling the way of its working, and therein its justification.[1]

What Otto means by his distinction between the blind forces of Nature and uncomprehended Mystery is not quite clear, but as we read of this catastrophe at the Ennobucht we are reminded of the description of the Chittagong cyclone in *Bhānumati*, and of what must be the feelings of so many in Bengal as they see their slight achievements ruthlessly swept away before their eyes. Consciousness of the numinous in Nature permeates much Śākta worship.

Progress in religion comes by the gradual rationalisation and moralisation of the cruder experiences of the numinous, though there always remains a non-rational element in men's consciousness of the divine. It must be admitted that, taken as a whole, Śāktism belongs to an early stage of religious development, but when it is studied along the lines which Otto's book suggests it is approached with more sympathy and understanding than has often been the case.

II. The Mother-Goddesses of the Mediterranean

The worship of Durgā and Kālī may be usefully compared with the cult of Mother-goddesses in the ancient Mediterranean world. In considering the possible extraneous causes of the rise of Śākta ideas, mention has already been made of certain possible contacts between the civilisations of Knossos and Egypt on the one hand and pre-Aryan India on the other. These are too vague and uncertain, however, to

[1] *The Idea of the Holy*, pp. 83–84.

have any theories built upon them. Nor is that really necessary. The worship of Mother-goddesses is an extremely widespread religious phenomenon, and in its development in other parts of the world affords several parallels with what seems to have happened within Hinduism. Friedrich Heiler, in his great book, *Das Gebet*, gives instances from every part of the world to show that the conception of God as Mother is as natural and ultimate as the conception of Him as Father.[1]

We may take as an example the goddess worshipped by the Semitic peoples. She had many names; to the Canaanites and Phœnicians she was known as Ashtoreth or 'Ashtart, to the Babylonians as Iśtar, and possibly to the Arabs as al-Lāt and al-'Uzza. She was generally represented as a female figure, somewhat short of stature, usually naked, with rounded limbs, the hands supporting the breasts. Macalister tells us that the figure on the terra-cotta plaques which he has found in Palestine is invariably ugly and crudely represented, always naked, and with the parts of the body associated with the functions of maternity exaggerated.[2] By both Greeks and Phœnicians she was identified with Aphrodite, whose attributes were, indeed, largely moulded upon those of 'Ashtart, and whose rites were many of them of Phœnician origin. Of the cultus not a great deal is known. Certainly there was connected with it much religious prostitution and other obscene rites, but it is only fair to admit that these things were not confined to the temples of 'Ashtart, nor to the worship of female deities.

There are traces of this worship in the *Old Testament*, though it seems likely that the texts have been worked over by later hands anxious to conceal these things as much as possible. The influence of the Semitic goddess cults on the Israelites has not always been sufficiently recognised. In Jeremiah's day we learn that the women offered cakes and

[1] *Das Gebet*, 4th edition, p. 142 f. Cp. Heiler, *Der Katholizismus*, p. 186, where, after admitting the connection of the Isis and Artemis cults and worship of the Madonna, he says, 'Aber im wesentlichen handelt es sich nicht um eine äussere Herübernahme, sondern um ein spontanes Aufleben einer Urform des religiösen Denkens.'

[2] *A Century of Excavation in Palestine*, pp. 278–79.

other sacrifices to a Queen of Heaven (Jer., XLIV, 17; VII, 18), who is in all probability to be identified with 'Ashtart. Scattered allusions in the prophetic writings and other evidence (which can be found conveniently summarised in Oesterley's essay in the volume, called *The People and the Book*) suggest that goddess cults were prevalent in Israel up to the eve of the Exile. The famous series of *papyri* found at Elephantine, in Egypt, although fifth century documents, give a vivid picture of the popular pre-exilic religion which the prophets denounced, and from these it seems clear that among the four subordinate deities, who were recognised by the Jewish colony in addition to Yahu, one certainly, and another possibly, were female. The significant thing is that, though the Israelites, in common with the other peoples of antiquity, worshipped goddesses, they alone abolished these cults, in spite of the fascination which they have always had.

The worship of the Mother-goddess in the Mediterranean world has two main points of contact with that in India which we have been considering. The development of the worship seems to have been very similar, and the same kind of character was ascribed to the goddess by her devotees. Under one set of names many different deities were worshipped. What seems to have occurred, around the Mediterranean, as in India, is the gradual identification of many originally unconnected local 'numina,' and their fusion into the cult of one great goddess. 'Ashtart is sometimes the tutelary deity of a city, and in consequence its protectress and champion, a war goddess. But she is also the goddess of fertility and reproduction, as appears strikingly in the myth of the descent of Iśtar into the underworld that she may restore to life her bridegroom, the Sun-god. She ranks as queen of the gods and princess of heaven and earth. She is identified, too, with the planet Venus, largely because in the astro-theology of the Babylonians the planet Venus was the star of Iśtar. All these aspects of her nature are retained as she travels westwards, sometimes one being more prominent than another, sometimes several being combined. In her developed Semitic form 'Ashtart was pre-eminently the goddess of sexual passion, but a philosophy could underlie her worship, just as in the case of Kālī in India. The following sentences from the work of the French writers, Perrot and Chipiez, might well have been written with the Indian goddess in mind:

> Comme la nature même dont se résumaient et se personnifiaient sous ce nom toutes les énergies, Astarté, vraie souveraine du monde, dans son activité sans repos, ne cessait de détruire et de créer, de créer et de détruire. Par la guerre et par les fléaux de tout genre, elle éliminait les êtres inutiles et vieillis; en même temps, par l' amour et la génération, elle présidait au perpétuel renouvellement de la vie.[1]

To Aphrodite, as to Kālī, only male victims were sacrificed.

[1] *History of Art in Cyprus and Phoenicia*, p. 69. Quoted by Driver, *HDB*, I, p. 171. Driver's whole article on Ashtoreth should be consulted, and also that by G. F. Moore in the *Encylopædia Biblica*; and that on 'Ashtart, by L. B. Paton, in the *ERE*, 1.

CHAPTER XI

SOME KINDRED RELIGIOUS PHENOMENA (B)

III. The Mystery Religions

Edward Sellon, of the Madras Civil Service, in various writings drew a parallel between Śākta worship and the Mystery religions of the ancient world, and he is commended by Woodroffe as having been 'right in his general conclusions.'[1] In the new edition of Chantepie de la Saussaye's *Lehrbuch*, Edvard Lehmann also notes in quite general terms the similarities.[2] A more close comparison proves very instructive. The Mystery cults were essentially Eastern in origin and outlook, and it is this that makes their contacts with Śāktism so many and so obvious. Both movements are difficult to investigate, and difficult to judge impartially. Contemporary evidence in each case needs careful sifting. As Angus says in his valuable book, *The Mystery Religions and Christianity*: 'In estimating ancient testimony we should remember that religious abuses in every age attract more attention than the virtues of everyday life; that the testimony of eyewitnesses and initiates deserves credence over that of outsiders; that the ancient *mystæ* observed their vows of secrecy with provoking fidelity; that these believers have been mostly judged on the evidence of their most prejudiced and often ill-informed opponents, with their own lips sealed.'[3] It has been the same in the case of Śāktism.

The Mysteries were systems of symbolism, which by means of myth and allegory and various sacramental acts quickened the emotions of the worshipper, and sought to provoke in him a mystical experience. Remark-

[1] *SS*, p. 64. [2] *Lehrbuch der Religionsgeschichte*, I, p. 98.
[3] op. cit., p. 236.

able idealising power was shown, for some of the rites, such as the bath in bull's blood (*taurobolium*), were extremely coarse and repulsive, and some of the myths, such as the Zagreus one in which Zeus is represented as seducing his own daughter Persephone, taken literally must have been offensive even to the people of that day. Yet in the Taurobolium, according to Dill, 'paganism made, in however imperfect a form, its nearest approach to the religion of the Cross';[1] and the Orphics moralised the Zagreus story into a symbol of man's composite nature, a union of evil or titanic elements and divine or dionysiac elements, liberation from the former coming by way of self-renunciation and re-union with God. With parallels like this in mind it is easier to understand how the end of the dance of Kālī upon her husband Śiva is explained as 'the awakening of the human soul to the realisation of its origin from God, forgotten in the tumult of human emotions.'[2]

The Mysteries were also systems of redemption. 'Life was threatened and made wretched by the tyranny of Fate, the caprice of Fortune, the malice of ubiquitous Demons, the crushing weight of Astralism, the dread of Magic, the deepening sense of sin (which was part of the Orientalisation of the Western mind), and the Mystery of Death.'[3] This whole religious movement has to be studied with the social and political unrest of the times constantly in mind, and also the devastating earthquakes and frequent famines, all adding to the many ills that 'made human life a hell.' Ramsay traces in interesting fashion the effect of the physical characteristics of Anatolia on the conception of Divine Power found among the worshippers of the Great Mother in that region.[4] We have already seen how important the climate and the social and political background in India has been in the development of Śāktism.

Śākta teaching in its fullness is revealed only after several stages of preparation by the candidate for initiation. Similarly the Mystery religions were systems of *Gnosis* with

1 *Roman Society from Nero to M. Aurelius*, p. 555.
2 Underhill, *Hindu Religious Year*, p. 106.
3 Angus, op. cit., p. 51; cp. pp. 225, 226.
4 *HDB*, Extra Volume, p. 122.

many grades, some of them crude and symbolic, but others with a more elaborate ceremonial and a more systematic theology. A *disciplina arcani* restricted the full benefits of religion to a secret society of initiates, and the vow of secrecy was so scrupulously observed that it is difficult to discover what actually did take place. Almost certainly the appeal of the ritual, as in Śāktism, was primarily to the emotions, and aimed at producing psychic effects by which the devotee might experience the exaltation of a new life, but there was also an effort at a rational philosophy. Ramsay, writing in detail of the religion of Phrygia, says:

> With all their ugliness the Phrygian Mysteries must always remain one of the most instructive and strange attempts of the human mind in an early stage of development to frame a religion, containing many germs of high conceptions expressed in the rudest and grossest symbolism, deifying the natural processes of life in their primitive nakedness, and treating all that veiled or modified or restrained or directed these processes as impertinent outrages of man on the divine simplicity.[1]

The essence of Anatolian religion, the same writer tells us,

> lies in the adoration of the life of Nature, that life, subject apparently to death, yet never dying, but reproducing itself in new forms, different and yet the same. This perpetual self-identity under varying forms, the annihilation of death through the power of self-reproduction, was the object of an enthusiastic worship, characterised by remarkable self-abandonment and immersion in the divine, by a mixture of obscene symbolism and sublime truths, by negation of the moral distinctions and family ties that exist in a more developed society, but do not exist in the free life of Nature.[2]

The Mother goddess Leto, who was the centre of this worship, had her chosen home in the mountains amid the undisturbed life of Nature, among the wild animals. Her special companions were the lions and the stags, the strongest and fleetest of animals. In reading about her worship one is constantly reminded of the goddess of the Vindhya mountains, so similarly conceived and so similarly adored.

Men entered the Mystery brotherhoods for many very different purposes. 'Many are the wand-bearers, but few are the initiates' was indeed originally an Orphic verse. The sensual and superstitious could find much to appeal to them,

[1] *Cities and Bishoprics of Phrygia*, I, p. 92. [2] *Ibid.*, p. 87.

so also could the educated, the ascetic and the mystic. 'The divergence in the point of view of the *epoptæ*,' says Angus, 'was easy because of the heterogeneous elements, or perhaps, rather, the various strata of religious history embedded in the Mysteries.'[1] We have already seen the same thing in the case of Śāktism. Four distinct stages in the history of the Mysteries have been traced, and Śākta worship passed clearly through the first three of them. There was a time when the Mysteries in their crudest form were not mysteries for initiates only, but were the religion of a whole pastoral or primitive agricultural people. In the worship of Indian village goddesses, now identified with Durgā and Kālī, survivals of this stage may be seen. There was, secondly, a period during which this primitive religion, with necessary modifications, was the religion of the lower stratum of population, which adhered to the worship of the deities of the earth and underworld, a stratum of aborigines who survived successive waves of conquest. We know, for example, that in the Minoan-Mycenean civilisation there was worship of a Great Mother or Earth goddess, with whom was associated a lesser male deity, and that the invading Aryans or Hellenes ultimately accepted this cult and placed Demeter beside the Olympian deities of the sky.[2] In India, the Dravidians of the south, and the Mongoloid peoples of Bengal, were a lower stratum who maintained the primitive rites, and in the end secured their recognition within the religious system of the conquering Aryans. Thirdly, there was a stage during which the Mysteries were the concern of private religious associations. 'These *thiasoi*, or *sodalitates*, though they represent what Gardner has called "Hellenic Nonconformity," did not necessarily refuse conformity with the national public worship, but found their chief religious activity in the small brotherhoods.'[3] Such cult associations were of great importance for the spread of the

[1] op. cit., p. 42.

[2] Cp. Angus, op. cit., p. 169 f. Demeter's closest Indian parallel is Annapūrṇā, 'Giver of nourishment,' now regarded as one of the forms of Devī. Cp. *Hymns to the Goddess*, pp. 106, 159, for two fine hymns, one attributed to Śaṅkarāchārya and one from the *Tantrasāra*; Wilkins, *Hindu Mythology*, p. 265; Glasenapp, *Der Hinduismus*, p. 142.

[3] Angus, op. cit., p. 44.

Mysteries, and for the religious history of mankind, since they stressed the personal aspect of religion, and also contained the germ of a new and better social order. The equality of the sexes was insisted on, and the distinctions between master and slave were not recognised. This third phase in the history of the Mysteries seems similar to that in which Śāktism at present finds itself, and the groups which practise *chakra-pūjā* may be compared with the brotherhoods just mentioned. At Śākta meetings men and women are present as equals, and 'on entering the circle of Bhairavī all castes are on an equality with the best of the twice born,' though it is significantly added, 'on leaving it they are again separated into castes.'[1] In the Imperial period the Mysteries entered their fourth stage of development; what were once local worships cultivated in private associations became universal religions; Śākta devotees may dream of such a change coming to their faith; but at present there is little evidence for it, and in the next chapter reasons for expecting a decline rather than a growth in the power of Śākta ideas will be suggested.

What are now generally recognised as the defects of Mystery religions may also be charged against the Śāktas. Angus suggests four main lines of criticism.[2] In the first place, the Mysteries were freighted with myths of primitive naturalism, which, however symbolically interpreted, were to most people suggestive of evil. He quotes Cumont's words:

> All go back to a distant era of barbarism and have inherited from the savage past a multitude of myths, the offensiveness of which might be dissimulated, but not suppressed, by a philosophical symbolism, and of practices of which all the mystic interpretations could but ill conceal the fundamental crassness, the survival of a rude nature worship.[3]

Such a comment rises almost instinctively to one's lips on reading Woodroffe's somewhat laboured interpretations of Śākta symbolism and Śākta customs. Secondly, 'the Mystery religions linked themselves with a pseudo-science, Astrology, and with a pseudo-religion, Magic, which contri-

[1] Quoted by Monier Williams, *Brahmanism and Hinduism*, p. 192 n. Cp. Gilmore, *AJT*, XXIII, p. 448.

[2] Angus, op. cit., Chap. VI.

[3] *Religions orientales dans le paganisme romain*, pp. 107–8.

buted to their popularity for a time, but undermined their spirituality by fostering debilitating credulity and imposing terror in religion.'[1] We have already noted how much of the Śākta *Tantras* are taken up with Magic and with the teaching of how power may be acquired by the use of spells and charms. Woodroffe appears as an apologist for this, and tells us that 'there is nothing wrong in Magic *per se*,' and that 'modern scientific investigation has established the objectivity of leading phenomena of occultism';[2] unless one is prepared to adopt this position, the close association of Śāktism with Magic must be regarded as something dangerous and degrading. It is noted, in the third place, that the Mysteries were an extreme type of religion, a reaction from the political faiths of Greece and Rome, but a reaction which failed to hold the social and mystical instincts of man in equipoise. Such a criticism can be made against Hinduism as a whole, and not merely against the Śākta sect. The personal aspect of religion has been stressed, and mysticism fostered, but the social side of life has been neglected and depreciated. Fourthly, it is to be observed that the vagueness of the Mysteries and their excessive emotionalism, their weakness intellectually and theologically, contributed to their ultimate failure. These things can be traced in Śāktism also. In some circles the Sāṅkhya philosophy is used as a background for the teaching; others take a more monistic view; but the main appeal is to the emotions and not to the intellect. The numinous side of religious experience is that which is uppermost, and there is danger of its being forgotten that 'to get the full meaning of the word holy . . . we must always understand by it the numinous completely permeated and saturated with elements signifying rationality, purpose, personality, morality.'[3]

The defects of the Mysteries, then, are among the defects of Śāktism, but it is worth noting that, in the opinion of J. D. Anderson, in its crudest forms Śāktism has been no worse than the society depicted in the tales of Apuleius, whose *Metamorphoses* Angus regards as 'the best single textbook

[1] Angus, op. cit., p. 249. [2] *SS*, pp. 53, 55.
[3] Otto, *The Idea of the Holy*, p. 113.

for the study of the Mysteries,' and that that society retained something of the administrative instincts of Republican Rome.[1]

J. W. Hauer, in his interesting essay, *Die Dhāraṇī im nördlichen Buddhismus und ihre Parallelen in der sogenannten Mithrasliturgie*, has carefully compared certain Mahāyāna Buddhist texts, which show a marked colouring of Śākta ideas, with the so-called *Liturgy of Mithra*, which Albrecht Dieterich published in 1903. Dieterich connected the Liturgy with the Mithra cult, but this view has not met with acceptance among scholars; Cumont and Angus think it probably based upon Hermetic literature, while Reitzenstein regards it as a strongly Hellenised redaction of Iranian ideas under Egyptian influence.[2] It seems clearly a syncretistic product. Beautiful prayers are interspersed with directions as to proper breathing, shouting and gesticulation. It is in many ways very like a *Tantra*. Hauer's careful analysis of the mystical syllables used in the charms shows not a single word that is the same in both the Greek and the Tantric texts, but it is the same type of religion that produced them, and if Dieterich's suggestion, that the *pudendum* was used in the Greek cult be accepted, then we have still closer similarities.

IV. The Worship of the Virgin Mary

One last group of phenomena which help to the understanding of Śāktism may be considered. It has already been suggested that one of the causes of the rise of Śākta ideas within Hinduism was the transfer to Devī, when the other gods came to be viewed in a philosophical manner, of that personal devotion which is the natural expression of most religious experience. Brahman was the Unknown, the Impersonal, the Inert; Śiva lay asleep like a corpse; Brahmanism was in danger of becoming a philosophy and not a religion; it was then that older beliefs, long held by the more primitive people,

[1] Article 'Assam,' *ERE*, I, p. 138; cp. Angus, op. cit., p. 261.

[2] Dieterich, *Eine Mithrasliturgie*, third edition, 1923; Angus, op. cit., p. 248; Reitzenstein, *Die hellenist. Mysterien religionen* (third edition, 1927), pp. 46, 169–91.

reasserted themselves, and the goddess secured a central position in the affections of men. A very similar development may be traced in the Catholic Church, during the fourth and subsequent centuries, in the increasing place given in worship and theology to the Virgin Mary. Rudolf Otto has noted that 'from the standpoint of comparative religion, it is very striking and remarkable that the worship of *śakti* in India became powerful, and forced its way into the higher cult, in almost precisely the same centuries as those in which in the West the worship of the Panagia, the Theotokos, the *Regina coeli* developed.'[1] In the case of Mary we discover a remarkable growth in ecclesiastical tradition and belief regarding her person, a growth which ended in the formulation of the doctrines of her perpetual virginity, her absolute sinlessness, and her peculiar relation to the Godhead, by which she is fitted for special and successful intercession on behalf of mankind. These doctrines, which even Catholic writers admit to be a development from the attitude of the first century A.D., indicate the position which Mary had come to occupy in the hearts of the faithful. The protests of a Nestorius only increased the popular movement in favour of the worship of the 'Mother of God.'

Some, at any rate, of the causes are not difficult to discover. 'The solution of the Aryan controversy,' says J. S. Black, 'however correct it may have been theoretically, undoubtedly had the practical effect of relegating the God man redeemer for ordinary minds into a far away region of "remote and awful Godhead," so that the need for a mediator to deal with the very Mediator could not fail to be felt.'[2] Friedrich Heiler emphasises these same considerations. B. H. Streeter further suggests that 'in epochs when the Gospels could be read by few, but when the Last Judgment, with Christ on the Judgment Throne, terrifically pictured on stone or glass, was always before men's eyes, it was perhaps impossible to

[1] *Vischnu Nārāyana*, p. 158.

[2] 'Mary,' *Encyclopædia Britannica*, XVII, p. 812. Dr. James Cooper, *ERE*, VIII, p. 476, dissents from this and other of Black's contentions, but himself gives no satisfactory explanation. See Heiler, *Die Hauptmotive des Madonnenkults. Zeitschrift für Theologie und Kirche*, 1920, p. 417 f.; *Der Katholizismus*, p. 183 f.

preserve the element of tenderness in the Divine without adoring Mary also as the Queen of Heaven.'[1]

There was at the same time the upward thrust of what Harnack has called 'Christianity of the Second Rank.' We have seen how ready the religious instincts of mankind are to pay homage, in grosser or more refined forms, to the idea of womanhood. Many of those who entered the Christian Church in the fourth century had been brought up within nature religions, which developed such instincts to the full. 'The comparative colourlessness with which the character of Mary is presented, not only in the canonical gospels, but even in the most copious of apocrypha, left greater scope to the untrammelled exercise of devout imagination than was possible in the case of Christ.'[2] Accordingly the cult of Mary developed, and, as Harnack says, 'at last it became possible to include in Christianity the recognition of that which had been most foreign to primitive Christianity—homage paid to sex, the sacred, the divine, in a female form.'[3]

Ramsay in his essay, *The Worship of the Virgin Mary at Ephesus*, has traced in detail how the nature rites of Asia Minor were celebrated within the Catholic Church.[4] The general comment which Harnack makes is worthy of note, because it is applicable, *mutatis mutandis*, to what happened in India in the case of the goddess:

> The history of the worship of Mary is throughout a history in which the superstitious religion of the congregations and the monks worked upwards from its dark foundations, and undermined theology, which reluctantly submitted; but on closer examination this is seen to hold good of almost all specifically Western Catholic practices and doctrines. The *παραδουις ἄγραφος*, the tradition, which is now claimed as the papal, that has existed *semper ubique et apud omnes*, is the common superstition which everywhere and always expressed itself in analogous forms. In this sense the Catholic position cannot be disputed, that the Roman Church is the church of stable, and yet at the same time living tradition. This tradition is stable because the lower religious instincts which are compounded of fear and sensuousness are stable; it is living because theology by its devices gradually legitimated these instincts.[5]

[1] *Reality*, pp. 283–84. [2] Black, op. cit., p. 813.
[3] *History of Dogma*, IV, p. 308.
[4] *Pauline and Other Studies*, p. 126 f.
[5] *History of Dogma*, VI, p. 313 n.

Apologists for Śākta worship sometimes take a similar line to that adopted by defenders of the Catholic tradition, and Harnack's words might have been written of the gradual recognition in Hinduism of the worship of Devī.

CHAPTER XII

THE IMPERMANENCE OF ŚĀKTISM

SOMETHING must be said in conclusion about the value of the three chief characteristics of the movement in Indian religion which we have been studying, its emphasis on the Mother idea in connection with God, its conception of the deity as Destroyer, and the attention which it pays to ceremonial and ritual.

The conception of God as Mother is common in the East. Individual Western mystics have spoken of the deity in this manner, but it has had a far stronger hold in the East, not only among primitive peoples but among the civilised and highly educated, who are prepared to justify it as a richer and truer description of God than the more common analogy of Father. 'Why does the God lover find such pleasure in addressing the deity as Mother?' asks Rāmakṛishṇa. 'Because the child is more free with its mother, and consequently she is dearer to the child than anyone else.'[1] Sister Nivedita (Miss M. E. Noble) relates how one evening, shortly after her arrival in Calcutta, she heard a cry in a quiet lane, and, following her ears, found it came from a little Hindu girl who lay in her mother's arms dying. The end came soon, and the poor mother for a time wept inconsolably. Then at last, wearied with her sobbing, she fell back into Sister Nivedita's arms, and turning to her said: 'Oh, what shall I do? Where is my child now?' 'I have always regarded that as the moment when I found the key,' says Sister Nivedita. 'Filled with a sudden pity, not so much for the bereaved woman as for those to whom the use of some particular

[1] *Life and Sayings*, No. 89. Cp. Tagore's use of the mother-concept in *Letters to a Friend*, e.g. p. 42.

language of the Infinite is a question of morality, I leaned forward. "Hush, mother," I said, "your child is with the Great Mother. She is with Kālī." And for a moment, with memory stilled, we were enfolded together, Eastern and Western, in the unfathomable depth of consolation of the World Heart.'[1] In his autobiography Keshub Chunder Sen can write: 'I looked up to the Father, but the inner mansions of the Mother had never been opened to me, and no one had told me the way to them. There was no poetry in my heart in those days. . . . I began religion with fear and trembling, but am now immersed in joy. First hardness, afterwards tenderness, the Father first, the Mother afterwards.'[2] Obviously the difference between Eastern and Western social conditions results in different connotations being given to the terms Father and Mother, but this alone would hardly explain the fascination which the Mother conception has in India, and particularly among the Śāktas.

Christianity has not neglected this aspect of religious experience quite so completely as at first appears. The main stream of Christian doctrine has throughout the centuries been very hesitant about adopting the Mother idea explicitly, but there are many traces of its influence. We have already considered, from another point of view, the rise of Mariolatry in the early centuries of the Christian era. In defence of the worship of the Virgin it is often suggested that, just as children feel that they approach their father with more hope of success if mother has been previously secured as an ally, so Catholics feel that they can approach God more confidently by way of Mary. Admittedly, in speaking of God, all language is figurative and inadequate, but we must believe that all the finest things in human nature have their perfect counterpart in the Divine Nature, and we are therefore right, so it is argued, in making an ideal of womanhood central in our religion.[3] The trinity of popular Catholicism, the Father, the Mother, the Son, is true to the instincts of the human heart.

The Mother-idea is also traceable in many references to

[1] *The Web of Indian Life*, p. 17 f. Cp. Robertson Nicoll, *Ian Maclaren*, pp. 8–9.

[2] Mozoomdar, *Life and Teachings of K. C. Sen*, p. 516.

[3] Cp. Heiler, *Die Hauptmotive des Madonnenkults.*, *ZTK*, 1920.

the Holy Spirit. In the Apocryphal *Gospel according to the Hebrews*, Jesus is made to speak of 'My Mother, the Holy Spirit,' and the phrase is quoted by Jerome and others of the Church Fathers.[1] The Hebrew word for Spirit is feminine in gender, and this may have influenced the conception. In early Syriac theology the Trinity becomes the Father, the Son and the Mother; the Holy Spirit is identified with the last of these.[2] Centuries later, the Moravians in prayer and preaching spoke of the third Person of the Trinity as 'the dear Mother.'[3] Such language has been revived recently in more restrained form. 'The operation of the Holy Spirit,' writes Dr. David Smith,

> is the creative energy of God alike in the physical and in the spiritual domain, alike in generation and regeneration; what is this but the Divine Ideal of Motherhood? . . . The Spirit's yearning and striving and pleading and comforting, what are these but the outgoings of the Mother heart of God?[4]

This seems akin, in underlying philosophy as well as in language, to the teaching of the more thoughtful Śāktas.

A similar series of ideas is to be found connected with the Church, which is often spoken of as 'the Mother of the Faithful.' The apostle Paul, in his letter to the Galatians (IV, 26), speaks of *ἡ δὲ ἄνω Ἰερουσαλήμ ἐλευθέρα ἐστίν ἥτις ἐστὶν μήτηρ (πάντων) ἡμῶν*, and his language has been copied and developed in realistic fashion. C. F. Andrews thinks that this conception will gain a new fullness when interpreted by Indian Christians, and that it will be the means of rescuing the great Indian ideal of Motherhood from the debasing associations which have often clung to it.[5] Whether this be

[1] See M. R. James, *The Apocryphal New Testament*, p. 2 f.

[2] Cp. e.g. the language of Aphraates, the Persian sage who flourished in the first half of the fourth century. Burkitt, *Early Christianity Outside the Roman Empire*, p. 37; *Early Eastern Christianity*, p. 88 f.

[3] Isaiah, LXIII, 13, was connected with the N.T. language about the Comforter, which was regarded as 'the Mother of the spiritual children of God.' Cp. K. F. Noesgen, *Geschichte der Lehre vom heiligen Geiste*, p. 229.

[4] 'The Divine Motherhood,' *British Weekly*, December 3rd, 1925.

[5] *The Renaissance in India*, p. 262.

so or not, it is important to note that here again in the West the Mother idea has found a place for itself.

An even more striking example may be noted, coming from circles outside those of organised Christianity. In his later works August Comte sought to bring back religion, which Positivism had banished, in the form of a sentimental worship of Humanity, symbolised by Woman, and in particular by the Virgin Mary. 'Women, as the sex characterised by sympathy, are the fit representatives of Humanity. They mediate between Humanity and man, as Humanity mediates between man and the world.'[1] Somewhat similar conceptions may be found in Benjamin Kidd's *Science of Power*.

Illustrations of this kind might be multiplied to show how widespread is the tendency to think in Mother-terms of the central facts of religion. 'Our sense of the Motherliness of God,' says Dr. Rendel Harris,

> increases as we get older. We arrive at the second childhood of old age, but in a good sense—a second innocence, a second simplicity, a second trust, that are even richer than the first. We say our *Paternoster* in the morning when the sun rises, but our *Maternoster* at night when the curtains are drawn.[2]

In all the great faiths save Hinduism, however, the tendency to use language of this kind has been carefully watched and checked, because men have discovered how liable it is to gain sentimental, if not sexual, associations. Modern Europe is possibly prudish to excess, but the general development of religious thought testifies to the dangers of Mother-symbolism. When the West speaks of God as Father, it is not thinking of Him as male rather than female, but as the ideal parent. The highest conception of Fatherhood contains within it the Mother ideal. Individual Śāktas have many noble things to say of God as Mother, but none that cannot be adequately translated into terms of the other analogy, and

[1] Edward Caird, *The Social Philosophy and Religion of Comte*, p. 32.

[2] *British Weekly*, February 24th, 1927. Cp. F. W. Robertson, *The Glory of the Virgin Mary, Sermons*, 2nd Series, for some judicious remarks on the whole subject. H. Wheeler Robinson, *The Christian Experience of the Holy Spirit*, p. 280, remarks that in some respects 'Motherhood' is a richer metaphor than 'Fatherhood.'

the literature of the movement as a whole affords a striking example of how difficult it is for such language to escape debasing suggestions.

The question of the use of erotic language to express religious experience is a large and important one. Here it is only possible to draw attention to one or two points suggested by the movement we have been studying. Many of the most famous of the hymns to Devī consist of detailed descriptions of the various parts of her body, on which the devotee is urged to meditate. The Western reader is reminded of the Hebrew *Song of Songs*, but there is this important difference. The Jewish work was almost certainly in origin a group of love-songs, later wrongly interpreted and allegorised into a picture of the relation between Christ and His Church. Christians have always been somewhat troubled about its position in the canon of scripture. The Śākta hymns, on the other hand, seem to have been quite deliberately written for religious purposes, though Woodroffe and others assure us that there is an esoteric meaning which is more important and more lofty than that on the surface. The Christian allegorised what his moral sense prevented his taking literally; the Śākta literalises and then justifies.[1]

The sexual language employed must not be too closely pressed. We are often reminded that in India the *liṅga* symbol is to a large extent free from unpleasant suggestions because of its familiarity. This can be the more easily understood when it is recalled how in other religious systems the baser associations of words and practices have gradually disappeared. The Hebrew verb 'to know' (*yada*), for example, had originally a sexual meaning, and this seems to be present in greater or less degree in the use of the word by a great prophet even, like Hosea;[2] but it gradually rose above such primitive usage, and became one of the richest and noblest Hebrew religious terms. The same is no doubt true of many Indian words and phrases which a Westerner

[1] Cp. Cave, *Redemption, Hindu and Christian*, p. 114 f., on the sensuality of the Rādhā-Kṛishṇa cult.

[2] Cp. Melville Scott, *The Message of Hosea*, where several difficult passages are interpreted as containing more of the old ideas connected with *yada* than has been recognised.

is inclined to interpret too literally. As Angus reminds us: 'In all religions rites become stereotyped and formulæ remain unchanged, while the interpretation and symbolism are constantly expanding in spirituality. . . . In pagan sacraments, as in the whole course of religious history, man's spirit marched painfully from sacramentarianism through symbolism to that goal to which the external symbol pointed in the truth of God.'[1]

It is possible, however, to underestimate the debasing effect of Śākta literature. The superior attitude, which urges that the really spiritual man can see a great truth in language which is dangerously exciting to the ordinary man, is no real excuse for the sensuality of much that is in the *Tantras*. Woodroffe does not carry conviction on this matter, though what he says is important and revealing evidence of his own standpoint.

> There is a good deal of what is called erotic symbolism in some of the *Tantras*. This is apt to shock many English people who are by no means all so moral in fact as some might think this sensibility suggests. It does not necessarily carry this suggestion to me. Such fear of erotic symbols is rather indicative, in the generality of cases, of a natural tendency to impurity and want of self-control. The great Edward Carpenter speaks of the 'impure hush' in these matters. A person whose mind is naturally bent towards sensual thoughts, but who desires to control them, has no doubt a fear, which one readily understands, of anything which may provoke such thoughts. But such a man is, in this respect, lower than him (*sic*) who looks upon natural things in a natural way without fear of injury himself; and infinitely lower than him to whom all is manifestation of the One Consciousness, and who realises this in those things which are the cause of all to the imperfectly governed *Paśu*. Nothing is in itself impure. It is the mind that makes it so.[2]

Even if we admit that to the pure all things are pure, there remain some things which are more expedient and more healthy than others.

Nevertheless, we do wrong to Indian religious thought if we do not recognise the freer attitude of Easterners to these things. A saying like the following, by Rāmakṛishṇa, is at first apt to seem blasphemous to Western ears, but on reflection is seen to be not without suggestiveness of a good kind. 'The

[1] *Mystery Religions and Christianity*, pp. 131–33.
[2] *SS*, p. 319 f. *Paśu* = the ordinary 'beast' man. See Chap. II.

knowledge of God,' he said, 'may be likened to a man, while the love of God is like a woman. Knowledge has entry only up to the outer rooms of God, but no one can enter into the inner mysteries of God save a lover, for a woman has access even into the harem (i.e. sacred or guarded place) of the Almighty.'[1] Even a Christian mystic like Sadhu Sundar Singh uses language which would sound strange, if not offensive, on the lips of a Westerner. 'The true mystic is one who lives with God; and very few, even of the greatest saints, have got very far in this. I am only a beginner, a child suckling milk from its spiritual mother. I enjoy it, and it gives me strength. I ask no further questions than to be his child.'[2] The image of the nursling he uses also when he speaks of prayer. Heiler has drawn attention to the further fact, however, that his sermons contain little of the Bride symbolism, so dear to some Christian mystics.

The second main characteristic of Śāktism is its conception of God as Destroyer, and its emphasis on the terrible and, in many cases, the revolting. There is a strong vein of pessimism running through Śākta teaching. It is arguable that a certain kind of pessimism has always marked the attitude of the choicest spirits towards the world; but there are different kinds of pessimism. That of the Hebrew prophets is ethical, and is based on their theory of duty, whereas that of most of the Hindu thinkers is speculative, and the consequence of their theory of being.[3] Among the Śāktas the more theoretical Indian pessimism is deepened by practical experience of dark social and political conditions. The more miserable has been man's lot, the more readily he has thrown himself, in all ages and climes, into the arms of a capricious destructive Power, an energy that creates only that it may once more destroy. Several instances we have already noted. Many of the *Old Testament* pictures of Yahweh have points of contact with Śākta descriptions, and were the product of similar upheavals and

[1] *Life and Sayings*, No. 172; Martin Buber, *Ekstatische Konfessionen* (Leipzig, 1921), a valuable collection of mystical utterances from many religions, gives this and other parallel sayings.

[2] Streeter, *The Sadhu*, p. 85; Heiler, *Sadhu Sundar Singh* (4th edition), p. 77.

[3] Cp. H. D. Griswold, *Brahman*, p. 64.

similar uncertainties. The apocalyptists had a faith in the sudden and terrible intervention of God, which was born of adversity and despair. Even in Christian times we find descriptions of Christ as dread Judge and Avenger, descriptions which must obviously be understood against a background of persecution and unhappiness. Much of the sternness of the Reformers' teaching, in particular that of certain of the narrower Calvinists, must be interpreted in the light of the social and political hardships which had been suffered. And it seems not irrelevant to note that the most recent and important movement in Continental theology since the War, that associated with the name of Karl Barth, is returning to a more awe-inspiring conception of God, as One before whom men must bow almost abjectly, even though He is the Father of the Lord Jesus Christ. There is a terrible Holiness, Majesty and Might about God, which separates Him by a great gulf from man, and once more emphasis is on His transcendence rather than His immanence. Keen observers regard this new trend of thought as, in part at any rate, due to the disillusionment and uncertainty caused by the sufferings which resulted from the Great War.[1]

Sir Alfred Lyall, in his preface to Sir Valentine Chirol's *Indian Unrest*, speaks of the 'incongruity between sacrifices to the goddess Kālī and high University degrees'; he wrote in 1910. The savage passions aroused by the War, and the belief of many in all the combatant nations that the only way to vindicate the righteousness of their cause was to sacrifice hundreds of thousands of lives, should have made us understand better the worshippers of Force in the East. It was not without justification that Tagore dedicated his passionate play, *Sacrifice*, published in England in 1917,[2] to 'those heroes who bravely stood for peace when human sacrifice was claimed for the Goddess of War,' for his protests against the lust for blood, which disguises itself under the form of devotion to a goddess, were not unneeded

1 See Adolf Keller, 'A Theology of Crisis,' *The Expositor*, 1925. Barth's *Römerbrief* and *Das Wort Gottes und die Theologie* can now be had in English translations.

2 *Sacrifice* appeared in Bengali 25 years earlier. Cp. Lily Dougall, 'The Worship of Wrath,' *Hibbert Journal*, 1923, p. 168.

in the West. A generation earlier, certain similarities in Eastern and Western thought had been noted. When Mazumdar returned from a visit to Europe, he told Rāmakṛishṇa that the philosophers were not atheists, as was commonly supposed, since they believed in an 'Eternal Energy—an unknown power behind the Universe';[1] he was referring apparently to Herbert Spencer's 'Infinite and Eternal Energy from which all things proceed.' Rāmakṛishṇa listened eagerly, and recognised in the Spencerian formula his own Kālī. More recently the teaching of Nietzsche has been interpreted as essentially the worship of *śakti.*

A study of the historical background of Śāktism has suggested that where the external conditions have improved, and life has become more stable and happy, there the more terrifying and objectionable features of the ritual have soon sunk into the background, and the sect has declined in importance. The rough parallels noted from the West confirm this impression. It is unlikely there will ever be a return to the terrible conditions of the sixteenth century, reflected in the work of Mukundarāma, and we may hope that the revival of fanatical Śāktism, in the present century, will be only a temporary phenomenon. Sister Nivedita recalls how she went once to Swami Vivekānanda with difficulties about animal sacrifice to Kālī. 'Why not a little blood, to complete the picture?' was his only direct reply.

> 'Fools,' he exclaimed once, as he dwelt in quiet talk on 'the worship of the Terrible,' on 'becoming one with the Terrible.' 'Fools, they put a garland of flowers around Thy neck, and call Thee "the merciful," and then start back in terror.' And as he spoke, the underlying egoism of worship that is devoted to the *kind* God, to Providence, the consoling Divinity without a heart, for God in the earthquake, or God in the volcano, overwhelmed the listener.[2]

In the West there have perhaps been times when men have adopted too familiar and benevolent an idea of the Deity, and have not realised that 'it is a fearful thing to fall into the hands of the living God,'[3] but one can guard against this

[1] For remarks by Mazumdar see Pratt, *India and Its Faiths*, pp. 61–62; Glasenapp, *Der Hinduismus*, p. 375.

[2] *The Master as I Saw Him*, p. 208 f. [3] Hebrews, X, 31.

kind of sentimentality without believing that the Universe is in the hands of a capricious and terrible power who demands sacrifices. That belief can never permanently satisfy men. Sooner or later they will exclaim, with one of the characters in Tagore's play: 'Let usbe fearlessly godless, and come closer to each other. They want our blood. And for this they have come down to the dust of our earth, leaving the magnificence of heaven. For in their heaven there are no men, no creatures who can suffer.'[1] And out of such defiance there may come a nobler and truer conception of God.

An attention to ceremonial is the third main characteristic of Śāktism. This side of the movement has in many cases degenerated into, or never risen above, Magic. As has already been noted, Eliot distinguishes this as Tantrism. It is a phenomenon wider than Śāktism, but the latter is practically nowhere found without it, though individual Śāktas, like Rām Prasād, have largely escaped its hold. All manner of rites are prescribed, and the most trivial details of life have all to be correctly performed, with the object of attaining supernatural power (*sidhi*), and ultimately of becoming united with the deity. In addition, in many of the *Tantras* there are instructions for sympathetic magic for the harming of enemies. Men seek salvation through correct ritual, in hardly intelligible rites, in attitudes and poses and gestures, in rosaries and images, in symbolic diagrams and the recitation of formulæ. In such mechanical proceedings there are things they can see and handle, things they can do, and by this means there does come to many a sense of power and peace. This side of Śāktism we are better able to understand in the West today than was the case fifty years ago, for here also we have witnessed a revival of ritualism. At its best, in both East and West, it is called 'Sacramentalism,' and it seeks to make all acts holy, to bring the divine near through the common things. All the details of life come within its ken. 'At the commencement of all rites let the believer say *Tat sat* (The One who is), and before eating or drinking let him say, "I dedicate this to Brahman."' Such an injunction from the *Mahānirvāṇa Tantra*, and the attitude to life which it implies,

[1] *Sacrifice.*

might be paralleled from many modern Christian books of devotion. At its worst, in both East and West, this attention to ceremonial is a crude Magic, open to all kinds of perversions, and dependent upon an unworthy and impossible conception of God. When material conditions give time for reflection, and scientific knowledge spreads, this trust in ritual will most surely disappear.

'Śāktism' is a universal religious phenomenon. In all the great religious systems of the world traces of its salient beliefs and attitudes may be found—belief in God as Mother and as Destroyer, and faith in the correct performance of ceremonies. Many of its practices in India, in Asia Minor, and even in Europe are remarkably similar, not because there has been direct borrowing, but because everywhere human instincts and passions are the same. In the West it is not found as an organised movement; only in an occasional rite or belief can the 'Śākta' attitude be traced. Better social conditions, the scientific spirit, and above all the changed conception of God which has followed the teaching and influence of Jesus Christ, have contributed to its disappearance. We may with some confidence predict that also in India, where it still has such a hold, it will be but a temporary phenomenon, and will gradually give place to a more rational and more healthy religious faith. There is abundant promise of this in the fact that within Śāktism itself there are to be found many expressions of deep and pure religious feeling. Some of these have already been quoted. The following *Baul*-song shows the heights which may be reached:

> If it had been merely words, would not Bhārata,[1] a worshipper through all the ages, would not Bhārata through *śakti*-worship have lost its power? Just tinsel ornaments and crash of drums, not in these is *śakti*-worship to be found.
> Offer the *bel*-leaves of a single heart, offer the Ganges water and lotus of devotion, and so perform your acts of adoration.
> You may give your sun-dried rice, you may give your sweetmeats, but do not think that with these you can gratify the Mother.
> Light the lamp of knowledge, offer the incense of an earnest soul: then only will that one who is divine fulfil all your desires.

[1] Bharata = India.

Wild buffaloes and goats, these are the Mother's children; she does not want them as a sacrifice.
If you would offer sacrifice, then slay your selfishness, and lay your love of ease upon the altar.
Kāñgāl[1] in anguish says: Where men make caste distinct from caste there can be no *śakti*-worship. Let all the castes be one and call to her as Mother, else will the Mother never grant us mercy.[2]

[1] Kāñgāl means 'poor' and is possibly the adopted name of the *baul* who wrote the song.

[2] *BRLS*, No. LXXXVIII.

BIBLIOGRAPHY

(Only the more important books and articles are given. Others are referred to in the footnotes. In Farquhar's Bibliography to *ORLI*, Section II, xi, is given to Śākta Literature. The more important *Tantras*, etc., are there named, but no work later than the *Śāktānanda-Taraṅginī*, i.e. about 1800.)

ANDREWS, C. F.:
The Renaissance in India. London, 1912.

AVALON, ARTHUR:
The Tantra of the Great Liberation (trans., intro., and commentary to the *Mahānirvāṇa Tantra*). Luzac, 1913.
Principles of Tantra (trans., intro., and commentary to the *Tantratattva* of Sriyukta Śiva Chandra Vidyanarva Bhattacharya). Pt. I, 1914; II, 1916.
The Wave of Bliss (trans. and commentary to the *Ānandalaharī*) Luzac, 1917.
The Serpent Power (trans. and intro. to the *Shatchakranirupana* and *Padukapanchaka*). Tantric Texts II, 1919.
Tantrik Texts, Vols. I–XI. London, 1913–22. (See also Woodroffe, Sir John.)

AVALON, ARTHUR AND ELLEN:
Hymns to the Goddess. Luzac, 1913.

BĀṆABHAṬṬA:
Harṣa-carita (trans. by Cowell and Thomas).
Chaṇḍīśataka (trans. by Quackenbos).
Kādambarī (trans. by C. M. Ridding).

BARTH, A.:
The Religions of India. E. T. Trübner, 1881.

BHANDARKAR, R. G.:
Vaiṣṇavism, Śaivism and Minor Religious Systems (G.I.P.A.). Strassburg, 1913.

BHAṬṬĀCHĀRYA, B. C.:
Indian Images. Pt. I., *The Brahmanic Iconography*. London, 1921.

BHAṬṬĀCHĀRYA, J. N.:
Hindu Castes and Sects. Calcutta, 1896.

Bhavabhūti:

Mālatīmādhava (trans. by H. H. Wilson).

Carpenter, J. E.:

Theism in Mediæval India. London, 1921.

Carthill, Al:

The Lost Dominion. London, 1924.

Cave, Sidney:

Redemption, Hindu and Christian. Oxford, 1919.

Chatterji, B. C.:

Kapālakuṇḍalā (trans. by H. O. D. Phillips).

Chirol, Valentine:

Indian Unrest. London, 1910.
India, Old and New. London, 1921.

Cowell, E. B.:

Trans. of part of Mukundarāma's *Chaṇḍī*, *JASB*, December, 1902.

Cowell, E. B., and Thomas, F. W.:

The Harṣa-carita of Bāṇa. Oriental Trans. Fund, 1897.

Crooke, William:

The Popular Religion and Folklore of Northern India. London, 1896.

Das, Govinda:

Hinduism.

Dubois, Abbé, J. A.

Hindu Manners, Customs and Ceremonies (1821, trans. and edited by H. K. Beauchamp). Oxford, 1906.

Eliot, Sir Charles:

Hinduism and Buddhism. 3 vols. Arnold, 1921.

ERE:

Articles on *Assam, Bengal, Dom, Durgā, Dravidians, Female Principle, Hinduism, Kalighat, Phalism, Rajput, Rāmakṛshṇa, Sāṅkhya, Tantras, Tantrism, Thugs*, etc.

Ewing, A. H.:

Intro. and analysis of the *Śāradātilaka Tantra*, *JAOS*, XXIII, 1902.

Farquhar, J. N.:

The Crown of Hinduism. Oxford, 1906.
Modern Religious Movements in India. Macmillan, New York, 1919.
Outline of the Religious Literature of India. Oxford, 1920.

FOY, W.:
Uber das indische Yoni-Symbol. Aufsätze zur Kultur- und Sprachgeschichte (Festschrift Kuhn). Munich, 1916.

FRAZER, R. W.:
Literary History of India. London.

FULLER, BAMFYLDE:
Studies in Indian Life and Sentiment. London, 1910.

GAIT, SIR EDWARD:
A History of Assam. Thacker, 2nd edition, 1926.

GHOSHA, PRATAPACHANDRA:
Origin of the Durgā Pūjā. Calcutta, 1874.

GILMORE, G. W.:
Tantrism—the Newest Hinduism. AJT, 1919.

GLASENAPP, H. VON:
Der Hinduismus. Religion und Gesellschaft im heutigen Indien. Munich, 1922.
Brahma und Buddha. Berlin, 1926.
Heilige Stätten Indiens. Die Wallfahrtsorte der Hindus, Jainas u. Buddhisten, ihre Legenden u. ihr Kultus. Munich, 1928.

GLASENAPP, O. VON:
Indische Gedichte aus vier Jahrtausenden. Berlin, 1925.

HAUER, J. W.:
Der Vrātya. Untersuchungen über die nichtbrahmanische Religion Altindiens. Vol. I. Stuttgart, 1927.
Die Dhāraṇī im nördlichen Buddhismus. Stuttgart, 1927.

HEWITT, J. F.:
The Tribes and Castes of Bengal, by H. H. Risley. *JRAS*, XXV, 1893.

HOPKINS, E. W.:
The Religions of India. Arnold, 1896.

HUNTER, W. W.:
Annals of Rural Bengal. 6th edition. London, 1883.

KEITH, A. B.:
The Sāṁkhya System. London, 1924.
The Religion and Philosophy of the Veda and Upanishads. Harvard Or. Series, 1925.

KENNEDY, M. T.:
The Chaitanya Movement. London, 1925.

KONOW, STEN:

Der Inder. Chantepie de la Saussaye's *Lehrbuch der Religionsgeschichte.* Vol. II. Tübingen, 1925.

KONOW, S., AND LANMAN, C. R.:

Rājaçekhara's Karpūramañjarī. Harvard Or. Series, 1901.

LOVETT, SIR VERNEY:

History of the Indian Nationalist Movement. Murray, 1921.

MACDONALD MSS.:

Yoginī Tantra (trans. by Munro).
Kāmadhenu Tantra (trans. by Munro).
Mantrakośa (trans. by Munro).
Tantrasāra (partial trans. by McCulloch and T. K. Chatterji).
Śāktānandataraṅginī (analysis by H. Anderson).

MACDONELL, A. A.:

Vedic Mythology (G.I.P.A.). Strassburg, 1897.
History of Sanskrit Literature. London, 1900.

MACKENZIE, D. A.:

Indian Myth and Legend. London, 1914.

MACNICOL, NICOL:

Indian Theism. London, 1915.

MACPHAIL, J. M.:

Kenneth Macdonald, M.A., D.D. London, 1905.

MAZUMBAR, B. C.:

Durgā, Her Origin and History. JRAS, 1906.
The Aborigines of the Highlands of Central India. Calcutta, 1927.

MOOKERJI, RADHAKUMUD:

Harsha. London, 1926.

MOZOOMDAR, P. C.:

The Life and Teachings of Keshub Chunder Sen. Calcutta, 1887.

MUIR, J.:

Original Sanskrit Texts. 5 vols. Trübner, 1873.

MULLER, F. MAX:

Rāmakrishna, His Life and Sayings. London, 1898.

NIVEDITA, SISTER (M. E. NOBLE):

Kālī the Mother. London, 1900.
The Web of Indian Life. London, 1904.
The Master as I Saw Him. London, 1910.

OTTO, RUDOLF:

Vischnu Narayāna. 2nd edition. Jena, 1923.

PARGITER, F. E.:
The Mārkaṇḍeya Purāṇa. Calcutta, 1904.

PHILLIPS, H. A. D.:
Chatterji's Kapālakuṇḍalā. Trübner, 1885.

PRATT, J. B.:
India and Its Faiths. Cambridge, Mass., 1915.

RADHAKRISHNAN, S.:
Indian Philosophy. 2 vols. London, 1923, 1927.

RĀJAŚEKHARA:
Karpūra-mañjarī (trans. by C. R. Lanman).

RELE, VASANT G.:
The Mysterious Kundalini. Bombay, 1927.

RIDDING, C. M.:
The Kādambarī of Bāṇabhaṭṭa. Or. Trans. Fund, 1896.

RONALDSHAY, LORD:
The Heart of Aryavarta. London, 1925.

RUSSELL, R. V.:
Tribes and Castes of the Central Provinces of India. London, 1916.

SEN, D. C.:
History of Bengali Language and Literature. Calcutta, 1911.

SLATER, GILBERT:
The Dravidian Element in Indian Culture. London, 1924.

SMITH, V. A.
Oxford History of India. 2nd edition. Oxford, 1923.
Early History of India. 4th edition. Oxford, 1924.

TAGORE, DEVENDRANATH:
Autobiography. Macmillan, 1914.

TAGORE, RABINDRANATH:
Sacrifice, and Other Plays. Macmillan, 1917.
Creative Unity. Macmillan, 1922.
Glimpses of Bengal. Macmillan, 1924.

TANTRIK TEXTS (edited by Arthur Avalon). Luzac, 1913–1922.

I. *Tantrābhidāna*, with *Vījanighantu* and *Mudrānighantu* (dictionaries of the single vowels and consonants of the Sanskrit alphabet with the Tantrik meaning. Introduction by Avalon.)

II. *Shaṭchakranirupana* and *Pādukāpañchaka*. Brief introduction by Avalon. (See *The Serpent Power*.) 1913.

III. *Prapañchasāra Tantra* (intro., analysis, and trans. of three hymns by Avalon). 1914.

IV. *Kulachūḍāmaṇi Tantra* (intro., analysis and trans. of one hymn by A. K. Maitra). 1915.

V. *Kulārṇava Tantra* (intro. and brief analysis by Avalon). 1917.

VI. *Kalivilasa Tantra* (intro. and summary by Avalon). 1917.

VII. *Shrīchakrasambhara Tantra* (a Buddhist Tantra, edited with intro. and trans. of Part I, by Kazi Dawasamdup. Foreword by Avalon, together with short summary of the general principals of Buddhism as given in the *Path of Good Wishes*). 1919.

VIII. *Tantrarāya Tantra*. Pt. I. Chap. I–XVIII. (Intro. and analysis by Avalon.)

IX. *Karpūrādistotra* (preface by Avalon, intro. and commentary by Vimalananda Svami). 1922.

X. *Kamakalavilasa* (a Kashmir Tantrik work; preface and annotated trans. of text and commentary by Natananandanatha). 1922.

XI. *Kaulopanishad*, *Tripurāmahopanishad*, *Bhāvanopanishad*, *Bahverihopanishad*, *Arunopanishad*, *Advaitabhvanopanishad*, *Kālikopanishad*, *Taropanishad*, with commentary by Bhaskararaya (intro. by Avalon). 1922.

THOMPSON, E. J.:

Krishna Kumari (Contemporary British Dramatists, No. X). London, 1924.

Tagore, Poet and Dramatist. Oxford, 1926.

THOMPSON, E. J., AND SPENCER, A. M.:

Bengali Religious Lyrics, Śākta. London, 1926.

TOD, JAMES:

Annals and Antiquities of Rajasthan. Oxford, 1920.

UNDERHILL, M. M.:

The Hindu Religious Year. London, 1921.

WARD, WILLIAM:

History, Literature and Mythology of the Hindoos. London, 1822.

WHITEHEAD, BISHOP H.:

The Village Gods of South India. 2nd edition. London, 1921.

WILKINS, W. J.

Hindu Mythology. Calcutta, 1882.

WILLIAMS, MONIER:
Brahmanism and Hinduism. 4th edition. 1891.

WILSON, H. H.:
A Sketch of the Religious Sects of the Hindus. Calcutta, 1846.
The Hindu Theatre.

WINTERNITZ, M.:
Geschichte der indischen Literatur. 3 vols. Leipzig, 1909–22.
Die Tantras und die Religion der Śāktas. Ostasiatische Zeitschrift, IV. 1915.

WOODROFFE, SIR JOHN:
Shakti and Shākta. 2nd ed. Luzac, 1920. (See also Avalon, Arthur.)

ZIMMER, HEINRICH:
Kunstform and Yoga im indischen Kultbild. Berlin, 1926.

INDEX